The
FIRST-TIME
HOMEOWNER'S
TAX GUIDE

An Essential Guide to Preparing Your Tax Return for a Maximum Refund

Robert L. Balducci

SPHINX® PUBLISHING
AN IMPRINT OF SOURCEBOOKS, INC.®
NAPERVILLE, ILLINOIS
www.SphinxLegal.com

First Edition: 2007

Published by: Sphinx® Publishing, An Imprint of Sourcebooks, Inc.®

Naperville Office
P.O. Box 4410
Naperville, Illinois 60567-4410
630-961-3900
Fax: 630-961-2168
www.sourcebooks.com
www.SphinxLegal.com

This publication is designed to provide accurate and authoritative information in regard to the subject matter covered. It is sold with the understanding that the publisher is not engaged in rendering legal, accounting, or other professional service. If legal advice or other expert assistance is required, the services of a competent professional person should be sought.

From a Declaration of Principles Jointly Adopted by a Committee of the American Bar Association and a Committee of Publishers and Associations

This product is not a substitute for legal advice.

Disclaimer required by Texas statutes.

Library of Congress Cataloging-in-Publication Data
Balducci, Robert L.
  The first-time homeowner's tax guide : an essential guide to preparing your tax return for a maximum refund / by Robert L. Balducci. — 1st ed.
     p. cm.
  Includes index.
  ISBN-13: 978-1-57248-645-4 (pbk. : alk. paper)
  ISBN-10: 1-57248-645-7 (pbk. : alk. paper) 1. Homeowners—Taxation—Law and legislation—United States—Popular works. 2. Income tax deductions—United States—Popular works. I. Title. II. Title: First-time homeowner's tax guide.

KF6535.Z9B35 2007
343.7305'23—dc22
                                        2007028754

Printed and bound in the United States of America.
SB — 10 9 8 7 6 5 4 3 2 1

3 9547 00300 6157

Dedicated in memory of Fabiana Balducci

Contents

Part I
PERSONAL RESIDENCE

INTRODUCTION

Deciding to buy a home is one of the most important decisions that you will ever make. You have to decide on the size, the location, the amount you are willing to spend, and so on. Such a large purchase can be a very frightening and stressful experience. However, if you are currently a renter, feel at ease knowing that buying a home is one of the smartest financial decisions you can make because there is no tax or financial benefit to ever renting—so if you are not reaping the benefits, guess who is? Your landlord.

As a homeowner, you can benefit from certain tax deductions not offered to renters. In addition, home investments have proven to return large rewards over time. Any Finance 101 class will tell you that real estate investments historically go up in value over time. As time goes on, your investment will be worth much more than what you paid for it. In fact, many of my clients have been able to cash out on their homes and retire comfortably on these types of investments.

This all sounds good, but buying and owning a home is no walk in the park. As with any investment, there are risks involved. Changing your lifestyle and becoming financially responsible to manage your investment can easily mitigate these risks. Therefore, before you decide to buy a home, you should realize that certain lifestyle changes will have to be made if you want become a successful homeowner.

Do you really know what you are getting into when you buy a home? There are many common events that all homeowners will eventually experience. For example, all home purchases will go through a closing, money will be borrowed, repairs will be made, and there will come a time to sell the home. This book is intended to provide you with the knowledge needed to become a successful homeowner.

Part I of this book is written for individuals who own a personal home or for anyone who has ever been interested in owing one. Part II is written for those individuals who own or plan to buy residential rental property. It can also be a useful tool for real estate agents, mortgage brokers, and real estate attorneys. You will meet these types of individuals during the home buying process. Some of these individuals may misinform you about home ownership, either intentionally for the sake of making a sale or unintentionally because of their lack of knowledge.

In any case, the goal of this book is to prepare you with what you need to know about home ownership. It accomplishes that goal by providing facts and real life experiences, and most importantly, it is written in plain English so it is easy to understand.

Chapter 1:

PURCHASING YOUR PERSONAL RESIDENCE

Purchasing a personal home should begin with planning. The best way to plan is to talk with other homeowners, educate yourself through books, and possibly consult with an accountant or certified financial planner. Learning from the successes and mistakes of others can ultimately save you money, time, and aggravation. Next comes the search for the home. Be prepared to be patient. One of the most common ways of finding a home is through real estate agents, whose job is to find the buyers of those homes that people want to sell. Be aware that the seller pays the agent for selling the home, so you should never pay a fee to anyone for finding you a home to buy.

Once you find that dream home, make an offer to the seller. If the seller accepts the amount you offer, the seller's attorney will formalize the deal with a sales contract. The sales contract will be forwarded to your attorney, so if you have not found an attorney yet, this is the time to find one. With most service providers, referrals are the best way to find a good attorney. However, always be wary of using the referral from anyone involved in the transaction, such as a real estate agent, mortgage broker, or seller.

Your attorney will review the contract, and barring any issues, the contract will be signed by all parties. The attorneys will then schedule a closing meeting.

Settlement Fees and Closing Costs

Once you decide on what type of home to buy, both you and the seller sign a contract. Then a meeting is scheduled with the seller, attorneys, and real estate agent to formalize the closing of the sale. At the closing, you, the buyer, sign an overwhelming amount of documents. In addition, you will be paying many fees known as *settlement fees* or *closing costs*. These fees can easily range from $15,000 to $25,000 depending on numerous factors, including 1) the cost of the home; 2) the amount borrowed; 3) your credit rating; 4) fees associated with acquiring the loan; and, 5) state and local laws. These fees, which must be paid at closing, are usually detailed in a closing statement known as a *Uniform Settlement Statement* (Form HUD 1). The buyer and seller are provided with a copy of the closing statement or HUD 1 at the closing.

Some fees that you may expect to pay at the closing include:

- abstract fees;
- legal fees;
- title insurance;
- appraisal fees;
- recording fees;
- transfer taxes;
- insurance premiums; and,
- survey fees.

Deducting Closing Costs

Many buyers believe that closing costs are tax-deductible when a personal home is purchased. While it is apparent that these costs may be very expensive, they are unfortunately not deductible on your personal tax return. Perhaps the confusion arises because closing costs may give you a tax benefit in the year that you sell the home (discussed in Chapter 3). Regardless, when you first buy the home, you cannot expect any tax benefit for the closing costs you have paid. Knowing this important fact before you purchase a home will ease the shock.

Points

To finance the purchase of a new home, most buyers turn to lending institutions, such as banks and mortgage companies. To negotiate a lower borrowing rate, lenders sometimes charge an up-front fee known as *points*. Each point charged usually equals 1% of the total amount borrowed. For example, if the buyer wanted to borrow $200,000 at an interest rate of 6%, but the bank was offering the loan at 6.25%, the borrower may pay one point (1% of the overall loan) to get the lower rate. In this case, the buyer is willing to pay $2,000 (1% of $200,000) to receive the desired interest rate of 6% on the $200,000 loan.

The amount paid for the point is considered to be pre-paid mortgage interest, and as you will learn in Chapter 2, mortgage interest is deductible when paid. Therefore, Uncle Sam generally allows you to deduct points in the year you purchase the home.

How to Deduct Points

To deduct points, the amount has to be paid at or prior to closing, and must be clearly identified on the settlement statement (Form HUD 1) as *points*, *loan origination fees*, or *loan discounts*. Lending institutions usually report deductible points to both the borrower and the Internal Revenue Service (IRS). You should receive a year-end mortgage interest statement (Form 1098) from the lending company specifying the amount of deductible points you paid. This amount should match the settlement statement you received during closing. Any discrepancies should be brought to the attention of the lender.

Helpful Hint

Lending institutions are required to report the amount of points paid by each taxpayer to the IRS; therefore, the deduction can easily be verified.

Where to Deduct Points

Enter the points reported on your year-end mortgage interest statement (Form 1098) onto Schedule A of your personal tax return, Form 1040. (See Illustration 1.1) You should note that the amount you pay for points is an *itemized deduction*. The IRS allows you to take either your total itemized deductions (e.g., charitable contributions, points, mortgage interest, real estate taxes, etc.) or the *standard deduction* (a fixed amount set by the IRS for taxpayers who do not have sufficient itemized deductions). Of course you would deduct the greater of the two amounts.

You should be aware that it is common for individuals who purchase their home at the end of the year not to be able to benefit from deducting the points they paid at closing.

Example:

On December 1, 2006, a young married couple, Joe and Mary, closed on their first home. They paid points of $5,000, which were clearly identified as loan origination fees on their settlement statement and the lender's year-end Form 1098. In addition, in 2006, Mary made a charitable contribution to her church for $250. They were not required to make any mortgage interest or real estate tax payments in 2006, since they closed in December. Joe and Mary had no other itemized deductions. Joe and Mary's total itemized deductions in 2006 were $5,250 ($5,000 in points + $250 in charitable contributions). However, the standard deduction for married filing jointly in 2006 was $9,500. Although Joe and Mary had valid itemized deductions, it would not make sense for them to itemize since the standard deduction was greater.

Alternative Ways to Deduct Points

If you do not benefit from deducting points in the year they are paid, as in the case of Joe and Mary, the IRS allows you to deduct them equally over the term of the loan. To calculate the amount that you can deduct each year, divide the points paid by the total months you will be paying back the loan.

Example:

In 2007, Mary and Joe paid $8,000 in mortgage interest, $2,000 in real estate taxes, and $75 in charitable contributions. So far their itemized deductions total $10,075. If the standard deduction is $9,500, than Joe and Mary's itemized deductions would be greater. Therefore, they would be able to take the itemized deduction. They can also add a portion of the points paid in 2006, since they were not able to use that deduction in the year they bought the home. Assuming they had a ten-year loan (120 months) Joe and Mary would be able to deduct an additional $500 [($5,000/120) x 12)] in points, allowing them a total itemized deduction of $10,575.

As you can see, Joe and Mary did not forfeit the points deduction even though they were not able to deduct them in the year they were paid. Of course, each taxpayer situation is different, and you or your tax preparer have to determine whether it would be best to deduct points in the year they were paid or deduct them over the life of the loan.

Non-Deductible Points

You should be aware that there are certain service fees charged by the lender that may be called points but have nothing to do with pre-paid mortgage interest. These fees can never be deducted on your tax returns. Examples are appraisal fees, preparation costs for the mortgage note, and mortgage insurance premiums. You should never see these amounts reported as deductible points on the lender's year-end 1098 statement. Do not confuse service fees with amounts charged for prepaid interest.

Moving Expenses

Your moving expenses are deductible if you start work at a new job location and meet certain requirements set by the IRS. The first requirement is known as the *distance test*. The IRS requires that your new job location be fifty miles farther from your old home than what your old job location was to your old home. (Your old home does not have to be a house; it can be a house, co-op, or apartment you rented or owned before the move.) For example, if your old home was seven miles away from your old job, the IRS requires that your new job be at least fifty-seven miles away from your old home.

The second requirement is called the *time test*. The IRS requires that you work full-time in the new job location area for at least thirty-nine weeks within the first twelve months. If you are self-employed the requirement is doubled (seventy-eight weeks within the first twenty-four months). These requirements limit taxpayers from deducting moving expenses, especially those individuals who just move down the street.

Types of Moving Expenses

If you meet the distance test and the time test, you may deduct reasonable moving expenses for traveling to the new home and moving your personal and household items. You may also include moving expenses paid for members of your household. Some allowable moving expenses include:

- lodging;
- shipping pets;
- plane fare;
- tolls;
- rental trucks;
- gasoline;

- shipping household items;
- storage during travel;
- shipping a vehicle;
- parking;
- packing supplies; and,
- packing and crating.

Helpful Hint

You are specifically not allowed to deduct the cost of meals. Also, remember to keep the receipts and records of all moving expenses.

Where to Deduct Moving Expenses

Deduct reasonable moving expenses directly on Form 1040 using supplemental Form 3903. (see Illustration 1.2.) You must also use Form 3903 to report any deductible moving expenses that your job reimbursed you for, because you can only deduct un-reimbursed expenses.

Deduct moving expenses in the year you pay them even if you have not yet completed the time test. The IRS allows you to take the deduction as long as you expect to eventually meet that requirement.

ILLUSTRATION 1.1

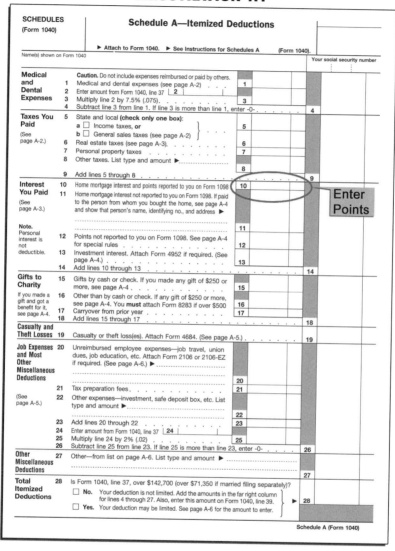

SCHEDULES
(Form 1040)

Schedule A—Itemized Deductions

▶ Attach to Form 1040.   ▶ See Instructions for Schedules A   (Form 1040).

Name(s) shown on Form 1040

Your social security number

Medical and Dental Expenses		**Caution.** Do not include expenses reimbursed or paid by others.	
	1	Medical and dental expenses (see page A-2) . . .	1
	2	Enter amount from Form 1040, line 37 [2]	
	3	Multiply line 2 by 7.5% (.075).	3
	4	Subtract line 3 from line 1. If line 3 is more than line 1, enter -0-.	4

Taxes You Paid
(See page A-2.)
	5	State and local **(check only one box):**
		  a ☐ Income taxes, **or**
		  b ☐ General sales taxes (see page A-2)
			5

	6	Real estate taxes (see page A-3).	6
	7	Personal property taxes	7
	8	Other taxes. List type and amount ▶.................	8
	9	Add lines 5 through 8	9
Interest You Paid (See page A-3.)	10	Home mortgage interest and points reported to you on Form 1098	10
	11	Home mortgage interest not reported to you on Form 1098. If paid to the person from whom you bought the home, see page A-4 and show that person's name, identifying no., and address ▶ -------------------------------- --------------------------------	11
Note. Personal interest is not deductible.	12	Points not reported to you on Form 1098. See page A-4 for special rules	12
	13	Investment interest. Attach Form 4952 if required. (See page A-4.)	13
	14	Add lines 10 through 13	14
Gifts to Charity If you made a gift and got a benefit for it, see page A-4.	15	Gifts by cash or check. If you made any gift of $250 or more, see page A-4	15
	16	Other than by cash or check. If any gift of $250 or more, see page A-4. You **must** attach Form 8283 if over $500	16
	17	Carryover from prior year	17
	18	Add lines 15 through 17	18
Casualty and Theft Losses	19	Casualty or theft loss(es). Attach Form 4684. (See page A-5.)	19
Job Expenses and Most Other Miscellaneous Deductions (See page A-5.)	20	Unreimbursed employee expenses—job travel, union dues, job education, etc. Attach Form 2106 or 2106-EZ if required. (See page A-6.) ▶......................... --------------------------------	20
	21	Tax preparation fees.	21
	22	Other expenses—investment, safe deposit box, etc. List type and amount ▶......................... --------------------------------	22
	23	Add lines 20 through 22	23
	24	Enter amount from Form 1040, line 37 [24]	
	25	Multiply line 24 by 2% (.02)	25
	26	Subtract line 25 from line 23. If line 25 is more than line 23, enter -0-	26
Other Miscellaneous Deductions	27	Other—from list on page A-6. List type and amount ▶......................... --------------------------------	27

Total Itemized Deductions	28	Is Form 1040, line 37, over $142,700 (over $71,350 if married filing separately)?
		  ☐ **No.** Your deduction is not limited. Add the amounts in the far right column for lines 4 through 27. Also, enter this amount on Form 1040, line 39.
		  ☐ **Yes.** Your deduction may be limited. See page A-6 for the amount to enter.
			▶ 28

Schedule A (Form 1040)

Enter Points

ILLUSTRATION 1.2

Form **3903**

Moving Expenses

▶ Attach to Form 1040.

Name(s) shown on Form 1040

Your social security number

Before you begin: √ See the **Distance Test** and **Time Test** in the instructions to find out if you can deduct your moving expenses.

√ If you are a member of the Armed Forces, see the instructions to find out how to complete this form.

1	Enter the amount you paid for transportation and storage of household goods and personal effects (see instructions)	1
2	Enter the amount you paid for travel and lodging in moving from your old home to your new home (see instructions). **Do not** include the cost of meals	2
3	Add lines 1 and 2	3
4	Enter the total amount your employer paid you for the expenses listed on lines 1 and 2 that is **not** included in the wages box (box 1) of your Form W-2. This amount should be shown in box 12 of your Form W-2 with code **P**	4
5	Is line 3 **more than** line 4?	

☐ **No.** You **cannot** deduct your moving expenses. If line 3 is less than line 4, subtract line 3 from line 4 and include the result on Form 1040, line 7.

☐ **Yes.** Moving expense deduction. Subtract line 4 from line 3. Enter the result here and on Form 1040, line 29 . . . . | 5 |

General Instructions

What's New

For 2004, the standard mileage rate for using your vehicle to move to a new home is 14 cents a mile.

Purpose of Form

Use Form 3903 to figure your moving expense deduction for a move related to the start of work at a new principal place of work (workplace). If the new workplace is outside the United States or its possessions, you must be a U.S. citizen or resident alien to deduct your expenses.

If you qualify to deduct expenses for more than one move, use a separate Form 3903 for each move.

For more details, see Pub. 521, Moving Expenses.

Who May Deduct Moving Expenses

If you move to a new home because of a new principal workplace, you may be able to deduct your moving expenses whether you are self-employed or an employee. But you must meet both the distance test and time test that follow.

Distance Test

Your new principal workplace must be at least 50 miles farther from your old home than your old workplace was. For example, if your old workplace was 3 miles from your old home, your new workplace must be at least 53 miles from that home. If you did not have an old workplace, your new workplace must be at least 50 miles from your old home. The distance between the two points is the shortest of the more commonly traveled routes between them.

Distance Test Worksheet

Keep a Copy for Your Records

1.	Enter the number of miles from your **old home** to your **new workplace**	1. _____ miles
2.	Enter the number of miles from your **old home** to your **old workplace**	2. _____ miles
3.	Subtract line 2 from line 1. If zero or less, enter -0-.	3. _____ miles

Is line 3 at least 50 miles?
☐ **Yes.** You meet this test.
☐ **No.** You do not meet this test. You **cannot** deduct your moving expenses. **Do not** complete Form 3903.

Form **3903**

Chapter 2

OWNING YOUR PERSONAL RESIDENCE

There are certain bills and expenses associated with owning a home that each owner should expect to pay. The biggest expense is the cost of the home itself. Since most people do not have hundreds of thousands of dollars in the bank to pay for a home, they borrow the money from a bank.

Another expense that you can expect to pay while owing a home is property taxes. Property taxes are assessed each year, and depending on where you live, this bill can be substantial. However, unlike a loan that eventually gets paid off, property tax bills live on indefinitely, meaning that as long as you own the home you must pay the annual property tax bill.

There are many more types of bills and expenses associated with owning a home. Some of these expenses are deductible and many are not. This chapter explains what types of expenses are deductible, how to deduct them, and what records you need to maintain. In addition, it addresses the special rules on deductions allowed by cooperative apartment and condominium owners.

Mortgage Payments

Most individuals finance the purchase of their home with mortgages through lending institutions. A *mortgage* is a promise to lend you money under the condition that you pay the amount back with interest. Lenders protect themselves in the event that you do not pay them back by securing interest (a *lien*) in the home. If you do not pay the loan back in a timely manner, then the bank can take the home away from you. In reality, you do not own your home until that mortgage is paid up.

Lending institutions require you to pay the amount you borrowed with interest in monthly payments. The total interest you pay depends on three things:

> 1) the *term* (length of time) of the mortgage;
> 2) the amount you borrow; and,
> 3) the interest rate.

The longer the mortgage term, the larger the amount you borrow, and the greater the interest rate means the more you will be paying back in interest. You should be aware that, in general, your monthly mortgage payments for the first few years mainly go to pay off interest. In fact, by the time you finish paying off the bank, your home will cost you two to three times more than what you originally borrowed. For example, if you take out a $210,000 mortgage for thirty years at a 7% fixed interest rate, by the time the bank is paid back, you would have paid them a total of $502,970, of which $292,920 would have been interest. This is not to mention those interest-only loans that are structured in such a way that you could literally never be able to pay them off.

Mortgage Interest

The IRS generally allows you to deduct the mortgage interest paid on up to two personal homes each year. However, the total amount borrowed must be less than $1,000,000. (If you file married filing separately, then the amount you borrow must be under $500,000.)

These restrictions appear to have been put in place to limit the amount of homes and interest wealthy individuals can deduct. The average taxpayers usually never come close to meeting these thresholds since they cannot afford more than one personal home or a home costing more than $1,000,000.

However, if you are one of those fortunate individuals who can afford having loans totaling more than $1,000,000, go to the IRS website at **www.irs.gov** and use the worksheets included in Publication 936, "Home Mortgage Interest Deduction," to determine the amount of interest that is deductible.

The amount of interest you pay each year will be reported to you and the IRS on a year-end statement Form 1098, and you will use this information on your personal tax return.

Helpful Hint

Lending institutions are required to report the amount of interest paid by each taxpayer to the IRS; therefore, the deduction can easily be verified.

Mortgage Interest Credit

There are certain state and local programs that offer a special tax credit to low-income individuals purchasing a home. To participate in this program, you must get a *Mortgage Credit Certificate* from your state or local government agency before obtaining a mortgage and purchasing a home. Be aware that some lending institutions help you obtain this certificate while processing your loan.

The *mortgage interest credit* can be taken each year on your personal 1040 tax return using Form 8396. The credit is usually a fixed percent (shown on the Mortgage Credit Certificate) of the mortgage interest paid during the year. The credit cannot be more than $2,000. One downside to taking the credit is that if you sell your home within nine years you may have to pay back all or some of the tax benefit you received under the program.

Another problem with the credit is that very few state and local governments participate in the program. Contact your state or local housing finance agency and inquire with your lender to see if the program is offered in your area.

Real Estate Taxes

Usually included in your mortgage payments is an amount for real estate taxes. Each year your state or local government requires you to pay real estate taxes based on the assessed value of your home. These taxes help pay for local schools, police, and sanitation. The government has the ability to place a lien on the property if your real estate tax payments become delinquent. This is why lending institutions usually require that you pay real estate taxes through them. Lenders collect real estate taxes in your monthly mortgage payments, deposit them in an escrow account, and pay the tax bill on your behalf when it becomes due.

The IRS allows you to deduct the real estate taxes you paid. Lenders will send you a year-end statement indicating the amount of real estate taxes paid during the year. If you pay real estate taxes directly, remember to keep records on the amount paid so you can deduct them at the end of the year.

Where to Deduct Interest and Real Estate Taxes

Enter the amount of interest from your year-end statement (Form 1098) and the real estate taxes paid on Schedule A of your tax return, Form 1040. (see Illustration 2.1.) Like points, interest and real estate taxes are itemized deductions. Therefore, your total itemized deductions must be greater than your standard deduction for you to benefit from itemizing your deductions. A detailed discussion on itemized deductions can be found on page 8.

Repairs and Improvements

One of the biggest expenses in owning a home is the cost associated with its upkeep. The IRS characterizes what is fixed in the home as either a repair or an improvement. Be aware that in either case the IRS does not allow you to immediately deduct any expenses for fixing your personal home. However, it is important that you understand the difference between a repair and an improvement because you are allowed to receive a future tax benefit for the costs associated with improvements when the home is sold. As you will see in Chapter 3, the IRS's consideration of the total amount paid for improvements may save you a substantial amount of money.

For now, understand the difference between a repair and an improvement and keep all the records to support all the improvements done on the home.

Repairs vs. Improvements

The IRS defines a *repair* as an expense that keeps the home in good working condition. For example, if your kitchen faucet is leaking and you have to replace the handle to get it to properly work again, then the IRS considers the expense a repair. Other examples of repairs include repainting the inside and outside of the home, fixing the gutters and floors, and repairing leaks and plastering. These expenses are needed to keep the home in good working condition.

However, not everything you fix in your home is a repair. If you put in a new kitchen or bathroom, or replace all the windows in your home, these types of expenses are called improvements. Specifically, the IRS defines an *improvement* as an expense that adds value to the home, extends the useful life of what was improved, or adapts to new uses in the home. Some examples of such improvements include the following.

- You remove the old linoleum from your kitchen floor and replace it with modern marble tiles; this adds value to the home.

- You replace the old tar and paper roof with a new longer-lasting rubber roof; this extends the useful life of the roof.
- You add a room in your unfinished basement; this adapts the home to new uses.

Other examples of improvements include adding a garage, installing a central air and heating system, installing a pool, insulating your home, and putting in wall-to-wall carpeting. As you can see, improvements are usually large and expensive jobs, which are probably not needed to keep the home in good working condition.

Records You Need to Maintain

Because you may receive a tax benefit for the amount you spend on improvements when you sell the home, it is important that you keep good records while you own the home.

The IRS has published a very useful recordkeeping table in IRS Publication 530 that will help you identify and track the many different types of improvements that you may encounter while owning your home. (see Illustration 2.2.) In addition to maintaining the table, you must retain all the receipts associated with the improvements.

Only keep records on improvements that still exist in the home. For example, if you installed a deck five years ago but had to replace it because it was unsafe, you do not need to keep records on what you spent on the first deck. The IRS only recognizes the expenses of the second deck that still exists. The expense of the first deck will not be considered since it no longer exists.

Home Improvement Loans

Improvements can be very costly, which is why lenders offer home improvement loans. As with any other loan, the bank charges interest on home improvement loans. You can deduct the interest on home improvement loans as long as the total amount borrowed (the mortgage and home improvement loans) do not exceed the $1,000,000 threshold discussed on page 17. Again, the amount of interest that you paid will be reported on Form 1098 by the lender. Deduct home improvement loan interest on the same line you deduct your mortgage interest.

Equity

The difference between what your home is worth and what you owe on the home is known as your home's *equity*. Earning equity is one of the reasons why it is better to purchase a home rather than pay rent. Over time the value of your home will increase and the amount you owe the bank will decrease, creating home equity.

Home Equity Loans

Lending institutions allow you to borrow on your equity as long as you pay them back with interest. These loans are referred to as *home equity loans*. Homeowners usually borrow on their equity to consolidate credit cards, student loans, or car loans, or to pay for other personal effects. Although this practice is common, it is not recommended to use your home as collateral for consumer goods. Nevertheless, the IRS allows you to deduct the interest on home equity loans. The loan generally must be the lesser of either the equity or $100,000 ($50,000 if married filing separately).

As with other deductible interest, lending institutions will report the amount of home equity interest paid on Form 1098. Deduct home equity interest on the same line you deduct mortgage interest.

Refinancing

For those of you who already own a home, you probably have received endless advertisements from lenders asking you to *refinance* your home (take out a new mortgage). Many of you may have already done so. Homeowners generally refinance to get lower interest rates.

Refinancing became especially prominent in the early 2000s due to the lowest interest rates in several decades. Many homeowners took advantage of refinancing their homes to reduce their mortgage payments or shave off the amount of years left on their loan. It is expected that refinancing will become popular again. Many recent homebuyers who have bought in this inflated market used high variable rates or interest-only loans to buy their homes. With these types of loans, if interest rates go up, so does the monthly mortgage payment. To stabilize these payments, many homeowners are willing to refinance to more conventional fixed payment mortgages.

The process of refinancing is similar to the one when you first closed on your home. You will have to sign another mortgage note, be issued another HUD 1, repay closing costs, and possibly repay points.

Deducting Refinanced Closing Costs

Remember that the IRS does not allow you to deduct closing costs, so you should look for ways to save on these costs. If you decide to refinance, try to negotiate with your existing lender because they may be able to save you money on the title charges, mortgage sales tax, and other fees. These savings can amount to up to two-thirds of the closing costs that another lender will charge you since the new lender would have to originate a whole new loan. You will find that your current lender will be more than willing to refinance the loan to keep your business.

Deducting Refinanced Points

The points you pay to refinance are not deductible in the year you paid them, unlike the points you paid when you first obtained your mortgage. Instead, the IRS allows you to deduct the points equally over the term of the refinanced loan.

There is an exception to the rule that you should know. If you use part of the money to improve your home, then you can deduct the portion of points that relates to the improvement in the year you paid them. The portion of points that does not relate to the improvement must be deducted equally over the term of the loan.

Example:

Mike refinanced his old mortgage, on which he owed $75,000, with a new ten-year loan of $100,000. He paid points of $1,000 on the new mortgage. He plans to pay off the old mortgage and use the additional $25,000 for home repairs. Mike is able to deduct 25% or $250 [($25,000/100,000) x $1,000] of points in the year he paid them. The remaining points paid ($750) must be divided equally over the term of the loan.

There is one last thing to consider about points when you refinance. If your old mortgage ends early because you refinanced or sold the home, the IRS allows you to deduct any remaining points relating to a previous mortgage. Going back to Mike's case, assume he was equally deducting points each year on a previous loan and before he refinanced there were points of $2,000 that he still had not yet deducted. Because his old mortgage ended early, the IRS allows him to deduct an additional $2,000. There is one kicker to this rule—the IRS does not allow you to deduct remaining points if you refinance with the same lender. Therefore, if you refinance with your same lender to save on closing costs, you will not be able to get a tax deduction for unused points. Usually the savings on closing costs heavily outweigh the tax savings on deducting the remaining points of an old mortgage. In any case, consult with your tax preparer or work out the numbers yourself before you make the decision on who to refinance with.

Cooperatives

Cooperative housing (better known as a *co-op*) is generally a building complex where the tenants own the dwelling through a corporation. Each tenant buys stock shares of the corporation, which then entitle him or her to indirectly own an apartment in the complex. Owning a cooperative is the same as owning any home in almost all aspects. For instance, when you purchase a cooperative apartment you are subject to a closing, you are allowed to take out a mortgage to pay for the cooperative, you are responsible for paying property taxes, and if you sell the co-op the same tax rules as selling any home apply. Therefore, almost everything in Part 1 of this book pertains to individuals who own and live in a co-op.

However, there is one very important and significant difference about owning a cooperative apartment that must be highlighted. Cooperative owners are responsible for paying a monthly maintenance fee to their own corporation.

Maintenance Fees

The amount of *maintenance fees* assessed on the tenants consists of mainly three factors. The first factor is mortgage interest on loans obtained by the corporation to buy, build, change, improve, or maintain the building. The fact of the matter is the corporation owns the building and you only own shares of the corporation. To finance the purchase and keep up with the maintenance and repairs of the building, the corporation has to take out loans. You as a shareholder are responsible to pay the interest on these loans. So in addition to the mortgage you took out to pay for your apartment (or stock shares) you are responsible for part of the mortgage interest paid by the corporation.

The second factor is the real estate taxes paid by the corporation. You as an individual owner are not solely responsible for the building's property taxes; the taxes are assessed against the corporation. However, you as a shareholder are responsible for your part of the property taxes, just like any other homeowner property taxes must be paid.

The last factor is the day-to-day operating expenses to run the building. These costs include electricity in common areas, salaries for custodians and doormen, cleaning, and so on.

Deducting Maintenance Fees

Maintenance fees are calculated by taking the total interest, property taxes, and upkeep costs, and dividing that total by the amount of shares owned by the tenants. This is usually done by a *certified public accountant* (CPA) hired by the co-op board.

The amount of monthly maintenance fees paid for mortgage interest and property taxes are deductible. It is no different from deducting mortgage interest and property taxes on a house. The amount of interest and property taxes paid through maintenance fees during the year will be reported to you and the IRS on Form 1098. The certified public accountant will send you a copy of the form. Deduct the interest and property taxes on Schedule A of Form 1040.

Condominiums

Unlike the owner of a cooperative apartment, who buys stocks in a corporation, the owner of a *condominium* actually buys one of the apartments within a complex. A condominium can be an apartment in a building or one of many single homes connected together within a privately owned community. Just like conventional homes or cooperative apartments, condominiums undergo the same buying, owning, and selling process.

The only difference with owning a condominium is that besides actually owning the unit, tenants share in the ownership of common areas such as sidewalks, parking lots, elevators, and lobbies. With ownership comes the responsibility for the upkeep of these areas. Dues or assessment fees are collected from condominium owners to pay for this upkeep.

Deducting Dues or Assessment Fees

Bluntly, dues and assessment fees are *not* deductible for condominium owners. Why? Think of it in the same context of repairs and upkeep of a personal home. The IRS does not allow anyone to deduct repairs or maintenance made on a personal home. Since dues or assessment fees are used to maintain common areas, the same theory applies.

ILLUSTRATION 2.1

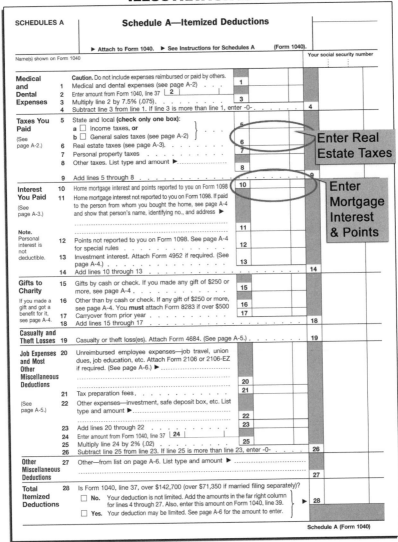

Schedule A (Form 1040)

ILLUSTRATION 2.2

Table 4. **Record of Home Improvements**

(a) Type of Improvement	(b) Date	(c) Amount	(a) Type of Improvement	(b) Date	(c) Amount
Additions:			**Heating & Air Conditioning:**		
Bedroom			Heating system		
Bathroom			Central air conditioning		
Deck			Furnace		
Garage			Duct work		
Porch			Central humidifier		
Patio			Filtration system		
Storage shed			Other		
Fireplace					
Other			**Electrical:**		
			Lighting fixtures		
Lawn & Grounds:			Wiring upgrades		
Landscaping			Other		
Driveway					
Walkway			**Plumbing:**		
Fences			Water heater		
Retaining wall			Soft water system		
Sprinkler system			Filtration system		
Swimming pool			Other		
Exterior lighting					
Other			**Insulation:**		
			Attic		
Communications:			Walls		
Satellite dish			Floors		
Intercom			Pipes and duct work		
Security system			Other		
Other					
			Interior Improvements:		
Miscellaneous:			Built-in appliances		
Storm windows and doors			Kitchen modernization		
Roof			Bathroom modernization		
Central vacuum			Flooring		
Other			Wall-to-wall carpeting		
			Other		

Chapter 3
SELLING YOUR PERSONAL RESIDENCE

For many of us there will come a time when we will sell our personal homes. We sell our homes because we retire and move to Florida, we sell because we move for a better job, or, sadly, we are forced to sell because we divorce or there is a death in the family. For whatever the reason, it is important that you are educated about the tax consequences from selling your personal residence. This chapter prepares you to succeed in benefiting from the most favorable tax laws on gains from home sales.

In the past, if you sold a home and were under the age of 55, you were required to buy another personal home of equal or greater value within a certain period of time or pay the gain on the home. This rule only postponed your gain to a later date. If you were 55 or over, the IRS allowed you to exclude up to $125,000 in gains, but this was only a one-time deal.

The 1997 Tax Relief Act

Then came the year 1997. Bill Clinton was president, the prices of homes were still low, and the interest rates were reasonably low. Any favorable tax laws on home gains at the time were too little too late, so of course the government signed the 1997 Tax Relief Act, which includes one of the biggest tax breaks on home gains. The problem was that with the low valuation of homes, many individuals could not benefit from these tax breaks.

In 1999, however, the real estate market began to turn around, as did the ability to buy homes with lowering interest rates. In fact, if you were one of those lucky individuals who bought in 1997 and 1998, you did not have to wait very long for your property to be worth more than double what you paid for it.

Excluding the Gain on a Home Sale

If you have been thinking of selling your home and you do not want to pay taxes on the gain, this chapter can tell you how. The 1997 Tax Relief Act allows an individual to exclude up to $250,000 gained on the sale of his or her main home. For married couples filing jointly, the maximum exclusion is $500,000. This means that you can walk away with $250,000 ($500,000 for married couples) in profit and not pay one single dime in taxes. This tax reform is a revolution in what some consider a tax-fueled economy. Unbelievably, many individuals are unaware of this tax law.

Who Can Exclude the Gain

To exclude the gain on the sale of your personal home, you must pass certain tests—the *ownership* and *use* tests. The home must be your main home and you must have owned and lived in it for at least two years during a period of five years from the date of sale. Single individuals can exclude up to $250,000 gain and married couples filing jointly can exclude up to $500,000 gain. If you own the home with another person, each of you can exclude up to $250,000 for your share of the home.

Meeting the Ownership and Use Tests

The ownership and use tests do not have to be continuous. Below are a few examples on how to meet the ownership and use tests.

Example:

Sue, a single parent, bought her personal home in February 2000. Sue decided to move in with her mother, so she sold her home in March 2002. She owned and lived in her home from the date she bought it to the day of the sale. Since Sue owned and lived in the home for at least two years, she can exclude up to $250,000 in gain.

Example:

Sue bought her home in January 2000 and sold her home in January 2005. She owned the home for the entire period, but she only lived there the first year and the third year, for a total of twenty-four months. The rest of the time she lived with her mother. Since Sue owned the home for at least two years and lived in the home for a total of twenty-four months within a five-year period from the date of the sale (although it was not continuous), she can exclude up to $250,000 in gain.

Married individuals can exclude up to $500,000 in gain as long as they meet the following requirements within a period of five years from the date of the sale.

- One of them must own the home for at least two years.
- Both of them must live in the home for at least two years.
- They must file a joint tax return.

Example:

Richard and Lakisha, a married couple, bought their main home in 1965 for $25,000. In 2001, Richard and Lakisha moved into a second home in Florida. In 2004, Richard and Lakisha sold their first home for $525,000. They file a joint tax return. Since Richard and Lakisha owned and lived in the first home within a five-year period ending in 2004, they are able to exclude up to $500,000 in gain.

Example:

Ronda bought a home in 1991 for $75,000. In April 2003, Ronda married her childhood sweetheart Jim. They have decided to live in Ronda's home. In May 2005 (more than two years later), Ronda sold her home for $575,000. Ronda and Jim file a joint tax return. Since they file jointly, at least one of them owned the home for more than two years (Ronda), and both of them lived in the home for more than two years, Ronda and Jim can exclude $500,000 in gain.

You should be aware that there is no limitation to the amount of times you can exclude the gain of your main home as long as you meet the requirements. However, if you exclude any gain from a sale, you must wait at least two years before you can exclude another gain.

Exceptions to the Ownership and Use Tests

If you sell a personal home and do not meet the ownership and use tests, the IRS will allow you to take a reduced exclusion on the gain if the primary reason you sold the home was because of a change of employment, health problems, or unforeseen circumstances.

To qualify for a reduced exclusion due to a change in employment, the new job location must be at least fifty miles farther away than the old job location to the old home. You must also own and live in the home while the change in employment occurs to be considered for the reduced exclusion.

The IRS will allow a reduced gain exclusion from the sale of your home if the reason for the sale was to treat or cure a disease, illness, or injury. The health problem is just not limited to you and your spouse. The IRS allows you to take a reduced exclusion if you sold your home because of health problems of the following family members:

- parent, grandparent, stepmother, or stepfather;
- child, grandchild, stepchild, adopted child;
- brother, sister, stepbrother, stepsister, half-brother, or half-sister;
- in-laws; and,
- uncle, aunt, nephew, or niece.

So if you owned a home for less than two years and had to sell it because you moved in with your disabled brother to care for him, the IRS will allow you to take a reduced exclusion on the gain.

Finally, you will be able to take a reduced exclusion due to unforeseen circumstances that you were not aware of before buying your home. The IRS defines the following as unforeseen circumstances:

- involuntary conversion;
- disasters, acts of war, or terrorism resulting in damage to home;
- death;
- unemployment;
- divorce or legal separation; and,
- giving birth to more than one child in a single pregnancy.

To determine the reduced amount on the exclusion of the gain from the sale of your home, go to **www.irs.gov** and use the worksheets included in Publication 523, "Selling Your Home" for the reduced exclusion calculation.

Determining Your Gain or Loss

To determine if you have a gain or a loss on the sale of your home, you must know the adjusted selling price and the adjusted cost (*basis*) of the home. The difference between the adjusted selling price and the adjusted cost is either a gain or loss on the sale of the home.

Adjusted Selling Price

The *adjusted selling price* is simply the amount you sold the home for, less any selling expenses. Some examples of selling expenses are commissions paid to real estate agents for selling the home, transfer taxes, and the fees charged by your lawyer for processing the sales contract and representing you during the closing.

Adjusted Cost

Determining the adjusted cost may be a little more involved but still easy to calculate. The formula for calculating the adjusted cost is simple addition and is as follows:

> Purchase Price (when you purchased the home)
> + Certain Closing Costs (when you purchased the home)
> + Capital Improvements (while you owned the home)
> = Adjusted Cost

The first thing you need to know when determining your adjusted cost is the purchase price of the home. The purchase price is simply the amount you paid for the home and can easily be located on the closing statement (HUD 1) that you received when you first bought the home.

Then add to the purchase price certain closing costs you paid when you first bought the home. Recall the discussion on the non-deductibility of closing costs in the year you purchase your home, and how some of these closing costs come into play when you sell the home. The IRS allows you to increase the cost of your home by adding certain closing costs to the purchase price of the home.

The closing costs you are allowed to add back are those fees you would have been required to pay if you had paid for the home in cash. Therefore, any closing costs associated with obtaining the mortgage would not qualify. Some of the closing costs that the IRS allows you to include in determining the adjusted cost of the home include:

- abstract fees;
- recording fees;
- inspection fees;
- legal fees;
- survey fees;
- transfer taxes; and,
- title insurance.

Most of these costs are listed on your old HUD 1 statement.

Lastly, add to the purchase price and closing costs any home improvements done while you owned the home. Recall the discussion in Chapter 2 that informed you those very expensive home improvements were not deductible, but that you should keep good records and maintain the table in Illustration 2.2 to account for the home improvements done while you owned the home because it would be relevant if you ever sold the home. The IRS allows you to add back home improvements to the adjusted cost (basis) of the home.

Review the table, which you should have been maintaining all along, and include all improvements made on the home. Refer back to Chapter 2 to refresh your memory on what improvements qualify.

Once you have completed the table, add the total amount of all the improvements to determine the adjusted cost of the home.

Inheritance

If you received the home through an inheritance, then the adjusted cost is generally the fair market value of the home at the time of death. The fair market value can be easily obtained through an appraisal. For example, if your uncle bought a house for $25,000 many years ago, and you later inherited it, the adjusted cost of the home would be the fair market value or appraised value at the time of your uncle's death. If the fair market value of the home is $500,000, the adjusted cost is $500,000. This special rule allows for huge tax savings at the time of sale.

Surviving Spouse

If you are a surviving spouse, your adjusted cost is half of the adjusted cost plus one-half of the fair market value at the time of your spouse's death. For example, you purchased a home with an adjusted cost of $100,000, and at the time of your spouse's death the house was appraised at $600,000. According to the rules, the new cost is $350,000—one-half of the adjusted basis ($100,000) plus one-half of the fair market value ($600,000).

Determining the Gain or Loss

Now that you know how to calculate the adjusted selling price and the adjusted cost (*basis*), you are ready to determine whether you have a gain or loss from the sale of your personal home. Simply subtract the adjusted cost from the adjusted selling price and the results will be either a gain or loss.

Example:

Leonard and Sue, a married couple, sold their personal home. Their adjusted selling price was $495,000. After working the numbers, Sue determined that the adjusted cost (basis) of the home was $395,000. Leonard and Sue have a $100,000 ($495,000 – $395,000) gain on the sale of their home.

Example:

Assuming the same facts above except that the adjusted cost (basis) of the home is $525,000, then Leonard and Sue would have a loss of $30,000 ($495,000 – $525,000).

Helpful Hint:

While it may seem that small fortunes are being made these days on home sales, I can clearly remember many individuals who suffered losses in the early- to mid-1990s from the sale of their homes. If the sale of your personal home results in a loss, the IRS will not allow you to deduct this loss.

The Tax on a Gain

If you determine that you have a gain on the sale of your home, then the next important fact that you need to know is whether it is taxable and how to calculate the tax. Determining whether it is taxable is simple. Remember, if the gain is less than $250,000 ($500,000 if you are married filing jointly) and you meet the ownership and use tests, then you pay nothing to the IRS as discussed earlier.

If the gain is more than the excluded amount or if you did not meet the ownership or use test, then you have to pay taxes on the gain. The tax rates on the gain of a personal home (*capital gain* taxes) have been changing dynamically during the last few years. These changes have resulted in low capital gain rates. For example, the capital gain rate in 2006 was 5% if your tax bracket was 15% or less, or 15% if your tax bracket was greater than 15%. Again, note that the capital gains laws have been changing frequently. Check IRS Publication 17 or with your accountant to get the latest information on the capital gain rates.

Helpful Hint:

The basic concept of capital gain rates is that the capital gain rate for property held one year or less (short-term) is higher than the capital gain rates for property held more than a year (long-term). Short-term capital gain rates are based on your regular income tax rate, but long-term capital gain rates have historically been lower. This means that if you have to sell your home, you do not qualify for the exclusion, and you know that a profit will be made, try to wait at least one year and one day before you sell the property. At least you may be able to benefit from the lower capital gain rates.

Where to Report a Capital Gain

Reporting the gain from the sale of your personal home has become very simple (so simple that when the IRS first changed the reporting rules in 1997, I called them up to make sure I was reading correctly).

If you do not have a taxable gain, then simply do nothing. The IRS does not require you to fill out any forms if there is no taxable gain.

However, if you have a taxable gain, report it on Schedule D of your Form 1040. Where you put it on Schedule D depends on whether the gain is short-term or long-term. Schedule D can be a difficult form to complete. Therefore, even if you are proficient in tax preparation, use reputable software to assist you in preparing the taxes. For those individuals who use a tax preparer, you still have to be educated and prepared with the right information so that your taxes can be properly done. The sale of a home is a very important tax transaction, and can cost you a lot of money in penalties and interest if you are caught not properly reporting a capital gain to the IRS.

Step-by-Step Illustration

Scott and Rita, who have been married for over twenty-five years, sold their home in July 2004. They have been living in the home since they first bought it in September 1993. They have been keeping a complete set of records on all home improvement done throughout the years on their home and have consistently updated the IRS recordkeeping table illustrated on page 29.

Step 1: Gather All Necessary Documents

They will need the following:

- closing statement or HUD 1 from when they sold their home;
- closing statement or HUD 1 from when they first bought the home;
- table of all home improvements (make sure it is complete);
- IRS Publication 523 (download this publication from **www.irs.gov**); and,
- copies of Worksheet 1, "Adjusted Basis of Home Sold," and Worksheet 2, "Gain (or Loss), Exclusion, and Taxable Gain," from Publication 523.

Step 2: Determine the Adjusted Selling Price

Scott and Rita reviewed the closing statement (HUD 1) they received when they sold the home. They extracted the amounts needed to calculate the adjusted selling price. They also looked at their checkbook to see if they paid out any other selling expenses that were not listed on the HUD 1. The following summarizes their adjusted selling price.

	Amount	**Information Taken From**
Selling Price:	$ 795,000	HUD 1
Less:		
Commission	$35,000	HUD 1
Legal Fees	1,500	Checkbook
Tax Stamps	7,900	HUD 1
Advertisement Fees	1,200	Checkbook
Total Selling Expenses	$ 45,600	
ADJUSTED SELLING PRICE:	$ 749,400	

Step 3: Determine the Adjusted Cost

Using IRS Worksheet 1, "Adjusted Basis of Home Sold," Scott and Rita figured out the adjusted cost of the home they sold. Scott pulls out the HUD 1 from when he first bought the home, copies of checks and receipts for some costs that were not listed on the HUD 1, and the Home Improvement Table that he kept updated while he owned the home. The following is a simplified version of Worksheet 1 for Scott and Rita.

	Amount	Information Taken From
Purchase Price:	$ 175,000	HUD 1
Add:		
Closing Costs		
Abstract Fees	$ 455	HUD 1
Inspection Fees	600	Checkbook
Legal Fees	1,500	HUD 1 & Checks
Recording Fees	150	HUD 1
Survey Fees	665	HUD 1
Title Insurance	1,575	HUD 1
Transfer Taxes	3,115	HUD 1
Total Closing Costs	$ 8,060	
Home Improvements	$ 35,000	Improvement Table
ADJUSTED COST	$ 218,060	

Step 4: Determine the Gain or Loss

Scott and Rita can complete Part 1 of IRS Worksheet 2, "Gain (or Loss), Exclusion, and Taxable Gain," or simply take their adjusted selling price less their adjusted cost to figure out if they have a gain or loss. The table below shows the result of Scott and Rita's home sale.

	Amount	Taken From
Adjusted Selling Price	$ 749,400	Step 2
Less:		
Adjusted Cost	$ 218,060	Step 3
GAIN	$ 531,340	

Step 5: Determine if You Qualify for the Exclusion

Scott and Rita meet the ownership and use tests discussed on page 32 because they have owned and lived in the home for at least two years within a five-year period from the date of sale (July 2004). In fact, they have been living in the home since they first bought it in September 1993, way over the time limit. Since Scott and Rita are married and file jointly, they will be allowed an exclusion of $500,000.

Step 6: Determine if Part of the Gain is Taxable

Scott and Rita completed Part 2 of IRS Worksheet 2, "Exclusion and Taxable Gain," to figure out what part of the gain is taxable. Below is a simplified version of Worksheet 2 that shows Scott and Rita's taxable gain.

	Amount	Taken From
Gain	$ 531,340	Step 4
Less:		
Exclusion	$ 500,000	Step 5
TAXABLE GAIN	$ 31,340	

Step 7: Report the Taxable Gain

Report taxable gains on Schedule D. In Scott and Rita's case, they had a taxable gain of $31,340. Since they owned the home for more than one year, the gain is considered long-term and should be reported on line 8 of Schedule D. On the next line they enter "Section 121 Exclusion" and subtract out the exclusion. (See Illustration 3.1 on how to report the gain.)

Helpful Hint:

You should remember the following items:

- *If there is no taxable gain after the exclusion, you do not have to report the sale.*

- *If you meet the ownership and use test, see if you qualify for a reduced exclusion.*

- *If you acquire the home through an inheritance or if you are a surviving spouse, follow the special rules to determine your adjusted costs.*

- *If you have to sell and believe there may be a taxable gain and do not qualify for the exclusion, hold the property for more than one year so that you can benefit from the long-term capital gains.*

ILLUSTRATION 3.1

Form 1040 — U.S. Individual Income Tax Return (for the year Jan 1 – Dec 31, 2004)

Label: SCOTT LEWITZ — 255-77-2278; RITA LEWITZ — 177-65-6688
Home address: 2525 OAK LANE, CLEVELAND OH 00010

OMB No. 1545-0074

Filing Status: 2 — Married filing jointly (X)

Exemptions: 6a Yourself (X), 6b Spouse (X); d Total number of exemptions claimed — 2

Income:
- 13 Capital gain or (loss) — 31,340.
- 22 Total income — 31,340.

Adjusted Gross Income:
- 36 Adjusted gross income — 31,340.

Transferred from Schedule D

Form 1040

ILLUSTRATION 3.1

SCHEDULE D		Capital Gains and Losses					12
(Form 1040) (99)		► Attach to Form 1040. ► See Instructions for Schedule D (Form 1040). ► Use Schedule D-1 to list additional transactions for lines 1 and 8.					

Name(s) shown on Form 1040
SCOTT & RITA LEWITZ

Your social security number
255-77-2278

Part I Short-Term Capital Gains and Losses — Assets Held One Year or Less

	(a) Description of property (Example: 100 shares XYZ Co)	(b) Date acquired (Mo, day, yr)	(c) Date sold (Mo, day, yr)	(d) Sales price (see instructions)	(e) Cost or other basis (see instructions)	(f) Gain or (loss) Subtract (e) from (d)
1						

2 Enter your short-term totals, if any, from Schedule D-1, line 2 . . . . **2**

3 **Total short-term sales price amounts.** Add lines 1 and 2 in column (d) **3**

4 Short-term gain from Form 6252 and short-term gain or (loss) from Forms 4684, 6781, and 8824 . . . . **4**

5 Net short-term gain or (loss) from partnerships, S corporations, estates, and trusts from Schedule(s) K-1 . . . . . **5**

6 Short-term capital loss carryover. Enter the amount, if any, from line 8 of your **Capital Loss Carryover Worksheet** in the instructions **6**

7 **Net short-term capital gain or (loss).** Combine lines 1 through 6 in column (f) **7**

Part II Long-Term Capital Gains and Losses — Assets Held More Than One Year

	(a) Description of property (Example: 100 shares XYZ Co)	(b) Date acquired (Mo, day, yr)	(c) Date sold (Mo, day, yr)	(d) Sales price (see instructions)	(e) Cost or other basis (see instructions)	(f) Gain or (loss) Subtract (e) from (d)
8	Home Sale Gain Realized	09/01/93	07/01/04	795,000.	263,660.	531,340.
	Section 121 Exclusion					-500,000.

Exclusion

9 Enter your long-term totals, if any, from Schedule D-1, line 9 . . . . . **9**

10 **Total long-term sales price amounts.** Add lines 8 and 9 in column (d) . . . . **10** 795,000.

11 Gain from Form 4797, Part I; long-term gain from Forms 2439 and 6252; and long-term gain or (loss) from Forms 4684, 6781, and 8824 . . . . **11**

12 Net long-term gain or (loss) from partnerships, S corporations, estates, and trusts from Schedule(s) K-1 . . . . . **12**

13 Capital gain distributions. See instrs **13**

14 Long-term capital loss carryover. Enter the amount, if any, from line 13 of your **Capital Loss Carryover Worksheet** in the instructions **14**

15 **Net long-term capital gain or (loss).** Combine lines 8 through 14 in column (f). Then go to Part III on page 2 . . . . **15** 31,340.

Schedule **D** (Form 1040)

ILLUSTRATION 3.1

Schedule D (Form 1040)   SCOTT & RITA LEWITZ   255-77-2278   Page 2

Part III   Summary

16   Combine lines 7 and 15 and enter the result. If line 16 is a loss, skip lines 17 through 20, and go to line 21.
     If a gain, enter the gain on Form 1040, line 13, and then go to line 17 below . . . . | **16** | 31,340.

17   Are lines 15 and 16 **both** gains?

[X] **Yes.** Go to line 18.

[ ] **No.** Skip lines 18 through 21, and go to line 22.

Transfer to 1040 line 13

18   Enter the amount, if any, from line 7 of the **28% Rate Gain Worksheet** in the instructions. . . . . ▶ | **18**

19   Enter the amount, if any, from line 18 of the **Unrecaptured Section 1250 Gain Worksheet** in
     the instructions . . . . ▶ | **19**

20   Are lines 18 and 19 **both** zero or blank?

[X] **Yes.** Complete Form 1040 through line 42, and then complete the **Qualified Dividends and Capital Gain
     Tax Worksheet** in the instructions for Form 1040. **Do not** complete lines 21 and 22 below.

[ ] **No.** Complete Form 1040 through line 42, and then complete the **Schedule D Tax Worksheet** in the
     instructions. **Do not** complete lines 21 and 22 below.

21   If line 16 is a loss, enter here and on Form 1040, line 13, the **smaller** of:

• The loss on line 16 or

• ($3,000), or if married filing separately, ($1,500) . . . . | **21**

Note. When figuring which amount is smaller, treat both amounts as positive numbers.

22   Do you have qualified dividends on Form 1040, line 9b?

[ ] **Yes.** Complete Form 1040 through line 42, and then complete the **Qualified Dividends and Capital Gain
     Tax Worksheet** in the Instructions for Form 1040.

[ ] **No.** Complete the rest of Form 1040.

Schedule D (Form 1040)

Chapter 4

HOME TAX AND ESTATE PLANNING

A home is more than just a place to live; it is a major investment that has to be nurtured. Proper planning before you buy, own, and sell your home can keep this investment healthy. Unfortunately, many homeowners make costly mistakes, from which some rebound and others do not. This chapter covers a few of the pitfalls that homeowners experience and guidance on how to avoid them, along with some estate planning tips.

Distribution from Retirement Plan

Many first-time homebuyers turn to their qualified retirement plans as a means to get money to pay for the down payment and closing costs needed to purchase a home. However, many individuals believe that they can simply take out money from their retirement plans without tax ramifications as long as the proceeds are used to purchase a home. It is not until they prepare their taxes that they come to realize the serious consequences from taking money out of their retirement plans. However, if done correctly, there may be a way to tap into your retirement plan without suffering serious consequences. It depends on whether you borrow or withdraw the funds, the type of retirement plan from which the funds are taken, and the amount taken.

Qualified retirement plans are complex tax code instruments that simply allow individuals to save money that ideally appreciates in value through investment strategies and earned interest, all of which is not taxable until you are eligible to withdraw the money. Qualified retirement plans include:

- pension, profit sharing, or stock bonus plans (including 401(k) plans);
- tax-sheltered annuity contracts;
- qualified annuity plans; and,
- individual retirement plans (IRAs).

Borrowing from a Qualified Retirement Plan

Generally, borrowing from a qualified retirement plan is treated as a taxable distribution, except if the loan is used to buy a home. This exception applies to all homebuyers, including first-time buyers, as long as the funds are used to purchase a main home. However, the maximum amount that you can borrow on a qualified retirement plan is the lesser of:

- $50,000 or
- half the present value (but not less than $10,000) of your non-forfeitable accrued benefit under the plan, determined without regard to any accumulated deductible employee contributions.

In other words, the loan must be the lesser of $50,000 or the plan value. Your administrator will let you know exactly what amount is available to borrow without having to pay taxes.

However, some individuals borrow over the allowed amount. When this happens, the person receives an IRS Form 1099R, "Distributions From Pensions, Annuities, Retirement or Profit-Sharing Plans, IRAs,

Insurance Contracts, etc." from the plan administrator. The purpose of the 1099R is to report to the IRS that a taxable distribution has taken place. The excess amount is reported in Box 1 and the distribution code L is reported in Box 7.

The tax consequences are very steep for any borrowing over the allowed amount. The distribution is taxed at your ordinary income tax rate, and an additional 10% penalty on the distribution will be owed if you have not reached 59½ years of age. The plan administrator is required to withhold 20% from the distribution to pay for what is owed. However, the 20% is usually not enough to cover the taxes and penalty.

Example:

Denise borrowed $30,000 from her retirement plan to purchase a main home. Because she had other loans outstanding, the amount she was able to borrow without paying taxes was only $10,000. She received a 1099R for $20,000 borrowed over the allowed amount. The plan administrator withheld $4,000 to pay for the taxes and penalty. Denise is in a 15% tax bracket. The 20% withheld is not enough to pay the taxes and penalties. Denise's loan will cost her a total of 25% of what she borrowed (15% tax bracket + 10% penalty). She is also responsible for state taxes on this distribution.

Depending on your tax bracket and state tax rates, an excess distribution borrowed from a retirement plan can generally cost you anywhere from 25–40% of the distribution. However, it is not a bad idea to borrow from your retirement plan if you need money to purchase your main home. The interest on the loan is usually low, the payback period is reasonable, and you do not lose a big chunk of your own money to taxes and penalties. Just do not borrow over the allowable amount.

Another reason why you would not want to borrow over the allowable amount is that the amount you borrow obviously has to be paid back. Returning to Denise's case, even though she paid the taxes on the $20,000, she is still responsible for paying back the loan to her retirement plan. Some individuals constantly borrow over the allowed amount, paying the taxes and paying back the loan. This does not make sense and is a waste of your money, so do not do it.

Withdrawing from a Qualified Retirement Plan

Simply withdrawing from a qualified retirement plan is never a great idea. Generally, withdrawing from a qualified retirement plan is treated as a taxable distribution, subject to ordinary tax rates and a 10% penalty. There is only one exception to this rule for individuals who are not at least 59½ and withdraw from their individual retirement accounts to buy, build, or rebuild a first home. However, this rule only applies to IRAs.

If you withdraw from an IRA and are under the age of 59½, the 10% penalty is waived. However, you are still responsible for paying the regular income taxes on the distributions. To qualify for the exception, you must be a first-time homebuyer and the distribution must meet the following three requirements.

1. It must be used to pay for the costs of buying, building, or rebuilding a home before the close of the 120th day after you received the distribution.

2. It must be used to pay for the costs of buying, building, or rebuilding a home for the main home of a first-time homebuyer who is any of the following:
    • yourself;
    • your spouse;

- your or your spouse's child;
- your or your spouse's grandchild; or,
- your of your spouse's parent or other ancestor.

3. All of your prior first-time homebuyer distributions cannot be more than $10,000.

Qualifying first-time homebuyers for the IRA exemption are defined by the IRS as individuals who have not owned a main home within a two-year period from the date the distribution is being used to buy, build, or rebuild a home.

Generally, all other distributions from qualified pension plans are taxable and reported on IRS Form 1099R, "Distributions From Pensions, Annuities, Retirement or Profit-Sharing Plans, IRAs, Insurance Contracts, etc." The distribution will be reported in Box 1 and the distribution code will be in Box 7. The tax consequences are very steep for withdrawing funds before age 59½. The distribution is taxed at your ordinary income tax rate and an additional 10% penalty on the distribution. Depending on your tax bracket and state tax rates, a withdrawal can generally cost you anywhere from 25–40% of the distribution. If you need money to help purchase your main home and have no other choice but the retirement plan, consider borrowing under the allowed amount as discussed on page 50.

Before You Refinance

Financial institutions such as banks make their money by lending money. As a matter of fact, financial institutions do quite well for themselves by lending you money. However, there are quite a few lenders and only a limited amount of borrowers, so to encourage business and company growth they have to lure existing borrowers to do business with them. Lending institutions accomplish this through their advertisement schemes. These companies make it very easy for someone to refinance.

Now that you know these lending companies' intentions, do not be persuaded to refinance just to refinance. Many people fall into the trap of refinancing their homes only to pull out some of the equity and extend their loan payments just because they were persuaded to do so. Let lending institutions work for you and do not allow them to get you to work for them. Have a good reason or need to refinance. Some such reasons include:

- obtaining lower interest rates;
- reducing the time period of the loan;
- obtaining a fixed payment loan;
- investing in other ventures; or,
- funding your children's college education.

There are a lot of factors to consider before you refinance. One is the closing cost. The refinancing process is very similar to when you first closed on your home. You will have to sign another mortgage note and repay closing costs. As you are aware, closing costs can be very expensive. However, if you decide to refinance, try to negotiate with your existing lender because they may be able to save you money on the title charges, mortgage sales tax, and other fees. These savings can amount to up to two-thirds of the closing costs that another lender will charge you since the new lender would have to originate a whole new loan.

You should weigh the additional closing expenses with why you refinanced in the first place. For example, if you refinance to obtain a lower interest rate, figure out the overall savings from the lower interest rate and compare it to the additional expense of the closing costs. Most people fail to make the comparison. Use an interest amortization table or your accountant to make the comparison. You will be amazed at the results.

Many people constantly tap into the equity of their home through refinancing. Every time they refinance, they lose money through the closing process. Your home should serve as a long-term investment. Constant refinancing defeats this purpose. Unfortunately, some homeowners barely pay off the loans when they sell their homes after so many years of owning it because of constant refinancing. Again, only refinance when you have good cause to do so.

Ideally, it is best to get a good fixed mortgage rate loan, pay off that loan, and (unless there is a good reason) never refinance. Your home will appreciate in value, eventually get paid off, and allow you to retire comfortably.

Trade Down

With baby boomers retiring, favorable capital gain tax laws, and the recent real estate boom, it is time to consider whether to trade down from your big home to a smaller one. As people get older and closer to retirement, health, family, and financial considerations have to be made in order to determine whether it makes sense to downsize from a large home to a more manageable one. Given the favorable tax laws for personal homes, now is a better time than ever to make your move.

The 1997 Tax Relief Act allows homeowners to exclude up to $250,000 ($500,000 for married couples) gained on the sale of a main home. To exclude the gain, you must meet certain tests— the *ownership* and *use* tests. The home must be your main home and you must have owned and lived in it at least two years during a period of five years from the date of the sale. Single individuals can exclude up to $250,000 gain and married couples filing jointly can exclude up to $500,000 gain. If you own the home with another person, each of you can exclude up to $250,000 for your share of the home.

The ownership and use tests do not have to be continuous. There is no limit to the amount of times you can exclude the gain of your main home, as long as you meet the tests. However, if you exclude any gain from a sale, you must wait at least two years before you can exclude another gain.

See Chapter 3 for the details of how to determine and report the gain. If the gain is more than the excluded amount, then you have to pay taxes on the gain. The tax rates could be as high as 15% and as low as 5%, depending on your tax brackets. Check IRS Publication 17 or with your accountant to get the latest information on the capital gain rates.

Reverse Mortgages

Ideally, when you retire, your home is paid for and your retirement income is sufficient to sustain your lifestyle. However, this is not always the case. Unfortunately, many individuals do not properly plan their retirements and find that the bills become greater than the retirement income. Even those who have a well-designed retirement plan find themselves in financial trouble because of family issues, health problems, and unexpected events. One option that is available to seniors who find themselves in a financial pinch is a reverse mortgage.

Reverse mortgages are programs developed by the federal government to assist and protect seniors and allow them to maintain their financial independence. Reverse mortgages allow seniors 62 or older to receive money from the equity of their home to pay off their current mortgage, health care bills, or home improvements, or to simply supplement their income. Reverse mortgages are great for those people who have substantial equity in their home but little liquid assets, such as cash.

The benefit of a reverse mortgage is that you keep the ownership rights to the home and do not have to make monthly payments to pay back the loan. The loan is paid back when you pass on, sell the home, or no longer use the home as your primary residence. In addition, the money is generally tax-free and does not affect your Social Security or Medicaid benefits.

The disadvantage of a reverse mortgage is its cost. Like any other type of mortgage, there are many closing fees associated with the loan, including service fees charged during the term of the loan. In addition, many reverse mortgage programs charge variable interest rates that may cause the amount owed on the loan to go up. Since reverse mortgage loans are paid when you pass on, sell the home, or no longer use the home as your primary residence, the amount owed can use up all or most of the equity of the home. This leaves very little for you in the case that the home is sold or is not a primary residence for your heirs in the case of death. Lastly, the interest imputed on a reverse mortgage is not tax deductible until the loan is partly or completely paid off.

Types of Reverse Mortgages

There are three basic types of reverse mortgage programs:

  1. single-purpose reverse mortgages;
  2. home equity conversion mortgages (HECMs); and,
  3. proprietary reverse mortgages.

The *singe-purpose reverse mortgage* generally has the least cost associated with it. However, this type of mortgage has a number of limitations. Some states, local governments, and nonprofit organizations only offer this type of reverse mortgage, and the proceeds can only be used for one purpose specified by the government or nonprofit lender. Generally, only low- or moderate-income recipients can qualify for this loan.

The *home equity conversion mortgage* (HECM) is a reverse mortgage federally insured by the U.S. Department of Housing and Urban Development (HUD). The fees charged for this type of reverse mortgage are sometimes very expensive, making it senseless for anyone staying in the home for only a short time. HECMs are widely available, the proceeds can be used for any purpose, and there are no income or medical requirements. The amount that you can borrow depends on your age, interest rates, value of the home, and the location of the home. Generally, the older you are, the lower the interest rates, the higher the value of the home, and the better the location, the more money you can borrow. Lastly, the HECM offers options on how the loan is given to you. Proceeds can be given in monthly fixed amounts, drawn down from a line of credit, or a combination of the two. HECMs are the most common of all reverse mortgages.

The *proprietary reverse mortgage* is a private loan backed up by private lending institutions. These reverse mortgages are similar to HECMs in that the fees are high, the loans can be used for any purpose, there are no qualification limitations, and you have options on how the loan is paid to you. However, HECMs provide a larger loan advance at a cost less than a proprietary loan. Given the costs associated with this loan, usually proprietary loans are given to homeowners who have a large equity value on the home.

Choosing the Right Reverse Mortgage

Before you decide to obtain a reverse mortgage, meet with a counselor from a government-approved housing counseling agency, talk with your accountant or financial advisor, and compare the options and terms offered on the loans.

Following is some general guidance to take into account in selecting a reverse mortgage.

- If you need money for a single purpose (such as home repairs or to pay your property taxes), have low income, and do not want to pay high closing fees, find out if single-purpose reverse mortgages are available in your area.

- If you feel that a single-purpose loan does not satisfy your needs and you would like to stay with a federally backed loan with flexible spending and funding options, consider an HECM loan. The rules and costs that lenders have to follow to process these loans will be the same no matter who processes the loan. However, the origination fee, servicing costs, and other closing fees may vary among lenders. Shop for competitive fees.

- If you have a lot of equity in your home, you may be able to obtain a proprietary reverse mortgage. However, because of the similarities to HECMs, it is best to compare which mortgage is most beneficial to your needs. A counselor will help you make this decision.

Where to Go for Help

AARP Foundation
601 E Street NW
Washington, D.C. 20049
800-209-8085
www.aarp.org/revmort/list

U.S. Department of Housing and Urban Development (HUD)
451 7th Street SW
Washington, D.C. 20410
202-708-1112
www.hud.gov/offices/hsg/sfh/hecm/rmtopten.cfm

Federal Trade Commission*
Consumer Response Center
600 Pennsylvania Avenue NW
Washington, D.C. 20580
877-382-4357
ftc.gov/bcp/conline/edcams/credit
*Click on "For Consumers," then "Mortgages & Your Home"

- Lending institutions and their employees make their money by lending you money and charging you fees. Unethical practices, fraud, and violation of laws sometimes occur. If you suspect such practices, notify the Federal Trade Commission.

Part II

Residential Rental Property

Chapter 5

PURCHASING YOUR RENTAL PROPERTY

While the IRS has several informative publications for personal homeowners, the publications available for rental property owners are not as helpful. Part II of this book is the simplest way to understand the tax implications of purchasing, owning, and selling rental property.

Part II of this book is written for the average rental property owner or for any individual interested in purchasing a rental property. This part can also equip real estate agents, attorneys, and mortgage brokers with the knowledge that a property owner expects them to have before engaging in any business transactions. Properly planned and managed, owning rental property can ultimately be a very profitable business. Unfortunately, with the attraction of profitability there are many misconceptions about investing in real estate. Part II of this book presents the facts about owning rental property while offering the information you need to know to successfully plan and manage your rental property.

An important word of advice is to read Part II from start to finish. Do not try to skip on to other sections without thoroughly reading each section in the order that it is presented. Certain basic concepts that will assist you in understanding what you need to know about owning rental property are introduced and explained in order. Therefore, if you skip to another section you may miss something that has already been explained.

Owning a Business

Owning rental property is similar to owning a business—you offer goods or services for money. All businesses have expenses associated with producing those goods and services. The difference between the money you collect (*income*) and the money you pay out (*expense*) results in a profit or loss. You must report these business activities and pay the applicable taxes to the IRS.

The basic business concept is very simple. If you generate income, you are allowed to deduct the related expenses. If there is a profit, then you must give the government its fair share by paying taxes. The concept of generating income and deducting expenses is more than simple—it is outright common sense. Would it be fair that you pay taxes on $100,000 of gasoline sales when your supplier charged you $80,000 for the gasoline? Of course not. Common sense says that you would only have to pay taxes on the profit of $20,000. These business activities—the amount of income earned, the expenses paid out, and the remaining profit or loss—are what you are required to report to the IRS.

Now correlate the business concept into rental property. As a landlord, you offer a service—apartment rentals—and in return you receive rental income. In offering this service there will be expenses that directly relate to generating the rental income. These expenses are mortgage payments, real estate taxes, legal fees, repairs and maintenance, utilities, and other necessary expenses. These business activities are reported on Schedule E, and the result, whether a profit or a loss, is transferred onto the first page of your personal tax return (IRS Form 1040).

The last thing you need to know about the basic business concept is how the IRS allows you to deduct business expenses. The IRS lets you deduct most expenses in the year that they are paid as long as they are ordinary and necessary. However, some expenses have to be deducted in a special method called *depreciation*.

Depreciation

Although too many lawyers and accountants use business jargon like "depreciation" to demonstrate their self-importance as a reason to charge their clients high fees, the fact is that depreciation is another important basic business concept in the accounting and tax world that must be understood if you want to succeed in any business venture, such as owning rental property.

In the tax world, *depreciation* is simply a way the IRS looks at certain expenses and tells you how and when to deduct them. Remember the basic business concept that if you generate income you are allowed to deduct the related expenses. While this concept may hold true, the IRS uses depreciation to control how and when you can deduct certain types of business expenses.

In the course of doing business you will purchase certain items that will have a useful life of more than one year. Since these items have a usefulness of more than one year, the IRS does not allow you to deduct the total expense in the year it is paid. Instead, you can only deduct a portion of the expense each year as prescribed by the IRS until the total cost is fully deducted. For example, you purchased a $2,500 laptop for the business. It is clear that the laptop will have a usefulness of more than one year. Therefore, the IRS will allow you to deduct only a portion of the cost each year until the total cost is fully deducted.

The IRS has a prescribed depreciation methodology it uses to determine how much and how long you can deduct the cost of those items that have a usefulness of over one year. This book will help you identify those depreciable expenses and will guide you on how to deduct them. Be aware that it is important to understand the concept of depreciation and know that you must adhere to the IRS's depreciation rules. In fact, the IRS is very strict on how you deduct business expenses because it is an area where people can manipulate the results of their tax returns.

The Cost of Rental Property

Investing in rental property is just like investing in any other business venture. Accordingly, there are many differences on how the IRS treats rental property over the way it treats personal home ownership. For instance, since the purpose of rental property is to produce income, many of the related expenses are deductible, which is not true of a personal residence.

The biggest expense in purchasing rental property is the actual cost of the property itself. The price of rental property depends on how many rental units the property has, whether the location is in an area of demand, the condition of the property, the mortgage interest rates, the economy, and so on. Whatever the price, the IRS will allow you to deduct the cost of rental property through depreciation. The IRS allows you to deduct the cost of rental property equally over 27½ years.

Remember that depreciation is simply the way the IRS tells you to deduct certain items that have a usefulness of over one year. The cost of rental property is one of those types of depreciable expenses. Consider why it makes common sense to depreciate the cost of rental property rather than deducting it in the year you purchase the property.

The first reason is that rental property is something that cannot be used up immediately like cleaning supplies. In fact, rental property can produce income for many years to come. Therefore, it would make sense to spread out the expense over the years that the property generates income.

Secondly, it would be absurd to take such a large deduction in the year you purchase the home. For example, if you bought a rental property for $500,000 and in the same year you earned $100,000, then you would have suffered a $400,000 loss. The reality is that you would not be able to benefit from such a massive loss in the year that you purchased the property. It is better to deduct the cost of the property over time to offset the future income that you will generate.

Helpful Hint:

Many people think they can simply deduct the mortgage payment of their rental property. This is not true. Mortgage payments are made up of many expenses that include interest, principal, and escrow amounts. Do not be concerned with the mortgage payment, because the cost of the property is being deducted through depreciation.

When to Deduct

The IRS allows you to begin deducting the cost of the rental property in the month the property is ready and available for renting. If you buy one of those handyman specials that needs a lot of work before it is ready to rent, then you have to wait until the home is available for renting before you can begin deducting the cost.

> ### Example:
> George bought a three-family home in July 2004 for $650,000. All three apartments needed substantial plumbing and electrical work to make them livable. In February 2005, George simultaneously finished the repairs on all three apartments, making them available for renting. In April 2005, all three apartments were finally rented. The IRS will allow George to begin deducting the cost of the rental property in February 2005, the month the property was ready and available to rent.

What to Deduct

There is a special rule that you need to know about deducting the cost of rental property. The IRS separates the cost of rental property into two parts:

> 1) the cost of the building itself (this amount is usually the greater), and
>
> 2) the cost of the land (the amount the IRS is most concerned about).

IRS rules have made it clear that the cost of land can never be deducted because land does not get used up, become obsolete, or wear out. This leaves rental property owners with a dilemma. Unless the building is hovering in thin air, every rental property purchased contains both the building and land.

There is a solution. There are two ways to identify just the cost of the building. As mentioned earlier, this amount is the only part that you are allowed to deduct through depreciation.

The first way to identify the cost of the building is simply to look at the sales contract. If the contract separates the amount of the building and the amount of the land, you are set. Only depreciate the amount of the building as stated on the sales contract.

If the amount of the building cost is not separated on the contract, then you must determine the building costs using real estate assessment values. You can make this determination through your property tax bills. *Property tax bills* are generally based on an annual assessment of both the land and the building. These assessments are usually detailed on a statement that is sent to you each year. To determine the deduction, take the building assessment amount listed on the statement and divide it by the total assessment of the entire property. The result will be a percentage, which you will multiply by the cost of the property. The formula is as follows:

[(Building assessment/total assessment) x total purchase price]

Example:

Return to the example of George's rental property on the previous page. As stated, he bought the property for $650,000. George would like to know how much of the cost he is able to deduct through depreciation. The contract did not state the building price, but he received his annual property tax assessment, which stated the building value was $450,000 and the land value was $50,000. He is allowed to deduct $585,000 [($450,000/$500,000) x $650,000].

No worry about separating the land cost with this one.

Helpful Hint:

Any expenses relating to the clearing, grading, planting, and landscaping of the land are generally considered land costs and therefore cannot be deducted. However, living in the northeast, I can make a very good argument that the $600 or so I spend each year for planting annuals on my rental property is deductible because the flowers die each year (become obsolete) and have to be replanted each season.

How to Deduct

The cost of your rental property has to be depreciated equally over 27½ years, and depreciation begins in the month the property became available for use. This section explains how to deduct the cost of your rental property.

Helpful Hint:

Calculating depreciation is just a mathematical exercise that can be done by any reputable tax software. I personally prefer using tax software because not only is it accurate, but it also maintains records of all depreciable activities. These records are especially needed when the property is sold.

The best way to depreciate the cost of rental property is to first determine the monthly depreciation amount. Simply take the cost of the building and divide it by 330 months (27½ years). However, in the first month that you begin to depreciate the rental property, you are only allowed to depreciate half of that month's amount. To illustrate, take a step-by-step look at George's case.

Step-by-Step Illustration

Step 1: Determine When to Deduct

According to IRS rules, you should begin to deduct the cost of rental property in the month the property is ready and available for use. As you will recall, George's rental property was available for renting in February 2005. February will therefore be the first month he will be allowed to begin depreciating the cost of the rental property.

Step 2: Determine What Amount to Deduct

Next you have to identify the portion of the purchase price that is attributable to the building. As you will recall, the rules do not allow you to deduct the cost of the land, so you have to separate the building cost from the purchase price. In George's example, the sales contract did not separate the cost of the building and land, so he had to use the tax assessment values to determine the building cost. George's calculation determined that he is allowed to deduct $585,000.

Step 3: Calculate the Annual Depreciation

Divide the total deductible amount by 330 months (27½ years).

Divide the first month by half.

Add the remaining deductible months for the year.

In 2005, George will divide $585,000 by 330 months to determine his monthly deductible amount of $1,773. George must divide the first month (February) by half ($1,773 / 2 = $887). Add $887 to the year's remaining deductible monthly amounts of $17,730 ($1,773 x 10 months). The 2005 deductible amount is $18,617 ($887 + $ $17,730).

In 2006, George will simply deduct 12 full months or $21,276 ($1773 x 12 months). George will deduct the same $21,276 for 2007, 2008, 2009, and so on.

Helpful Hint:

You generally must claim the correct depreciation deduction each year. You are not allowed to save depreciation deductions from one year to another. In addition, if you do not take the deduction, the IRS will calculate that a depreciation deduction was taken even if it was not. This is especially important when you sell the home. Therefore, to avoid any problems it is best to take the correct amount of depreciation deduction each year.

Settlement Fees and Closing Costs

The closing process for buying a rental property is the same as the closing process for buying a personal residence. Once you have decided on what home to buy, both you and the seller sign a contract and schedule a meeting with both of your attorneys, the real estate agent, and the bank representative to finalize the sale. At this meeting, known as a closing, many fees—such as settlement fees or closing costs—are paid by you the buyer. These fees may easily range from $15,000 to $35,000 depending on numerous factors, including:

- the cost of the property;
- the amount borrowed;
- your credit rating;
- fees associated with acquiring the loan; and,
- state and local laws.

These fees will be detailed in a closing statement known as a *Uniform Settlement Statement* (Form HUD 1). The lawyer provides the buyer and seller with a copy of the closing statement or HUD 1 at the closing.

Deducting Closing Costs

Unlike when you buy a personal residence, certain closing costs paid in connection with rental property are deductible. However, you have to add these closing costs to your purchase price and depreciate them over 27½ years. For example, going back to George's example we know that he is able to depreciate $585,000. If he had $10,000 in closing costs, he would add it to the $585,000 and would depreciate a total of $595,000.

The following is a list of closing fees that the IRS says you must add back to the purchase price of your rental property and depreciate:

- abstract fees;
- survey fees;
- legal fees;
- recording fees;
- title insurance; and,
- transfer taxes.

The IRS clearly states that you must depreciate the above list of expenses. However, there may be other expenses in connection with the purchase of the rental property. These expenses generally are deducted in the year they are paid. Chapter 6 discusses expenses related to rental property and how to deduct and report them.

Helpful Hint:

At the time of closing you may be required to pay into an escrow account funds to cover a few months of property taxes and insurance. Please note that these funds are on deposit and do not represent an expense. Therefore, you are not allowed to deduct funds that go into escrow. When the funds are used to pay for the property taxes and insurance, you will be able to deduct the amounts paid.

Chapter 6

OWNING YOUR RENTAL PROPERTY

The nature of owning rental property is to collect rent and pay the related expenses. This chapter will discuss what is considered rental income and detail the type of rental expenses that can be deducted. It will also guide you on where to report your rental property.

Rental activities are reported on Part I of Schedule E. This form reports the total rent collected and details the related expenses. The net result of the income less expenses is transferred to the first page of your personal tax return (Form 1040). An example of a typical rental activity is illustrated at the end of this chapter starting on page 90.

Please note that the rental activities normally reported on Schedule E are rentals of buildings, homes, apartments, or rooms. However, if your rental activities provide significant services such as maid services (e.g., a hotel), different reporting rules apply, which is not the subject of this book. Please refer to IRS Publication 334 for guidance on hotel-type rental activities.

Reporting Rental Income

Rental income paid by your tenants must be reported to the IRS when it is received. Rent is usually charged monthly and includes cash, checks, and any expenses paid by your tenants that you deduct on your tax return. Rental income must also include advance rent payments and payments received for canceling a tenant's lease.

However, security deposits that are to be returned to the tenant do not have to be included in rental income.

Simply report rental income received during the year on line 3 of Schedule E. Each property should be reported separately. You will notice that you can report up to three rental properties on the Schedule E form. Use additional forms if you have more than three rental properties.

Reporting Rental Expenses

Use IRS Form Schedule E to report ordinary and necessary rental expenses. *Ordinary and necessary expenses* are those that are customary and needed to operate your rental property. In the following discussion you will find guidance on the types of expenses incurred in the course of owing the rental property, as well as guidance on where exactly to report.

Advertisement

Advertisement is a good source of finding potential tenants. You may advertise in a local paper, produce flyers, or participate in some sort of Internet advertisement scheme. Whatever media used, you can deduct these expenses as long as they are ordinary and necessary. Deduct advertisement expenses in the year paid on line 5 of Schedule E.

Auto and Travel

In the course of managing rental properties owned in another state or locality, you are allowed to deduct ordinary and necessary travel expenses. These expenses include airfare, lodging, and 50% of your meal costs while traveling away from home.

For those individuals only a car ride away from their rental property, the IRS allows you to deduct ordinary and necessary auto expenses, including trips made to and from the hardware store.

There are two ways to deduct business-related auto expenses. The simplest is to take a *standard mileage allowance*. Just multiply the amount of business-related miles by the standard mileage rate published in IRS Publication 463 (you can download this publication from **www.irs.gov**). In 2006, the standard mileage rate was 44.5 cents. Therefore, if you drove your car 50 miles for the purpose of the rental property, you would deduct $22.25 (50 x 44.5 cents).

You can also use the actual method to calculate your auto expenses as discussed in IRS Publication 463. This method is not recommended because it is cumbersome and requires a lot of recordkeeping, which may not be worth the effort.

Deduct the total travel and auto expenses in the year paid on line 6 of Schedule E. Any reputable tax software will make the process of reporting auto expenses easy.

Helpful Hint:

The IRS requires you to keep records of all your expenses, including proof of mileage to claim the standard mileage rate. The simplest way to keep accurate records is to maintain a diary in the car. For each day you use the car for rental purposes, log in the destination, the total miles driven, and the purpose.

Cleaning and Maintenance

You should maintain your rental property so it is clean and well-operating. There will be certain expenses for snow removal and cleaning the property. You may even pay an individual such as a superintendent or caretaker to take care the property. Deduct these types of expenses in the year paid on line 7 of Schedule E.

Commissions

Line 8 of IRS Schedule E is typically used when commissions are paid for collecting rents or leasing the property. This is not a common type of expense, especially for individuals who own a small number of properties.

Insurance

To protect your property from loss, you will need to obtain property and casualty insurance, which are deductible expenses for rental properties. For properties close to the water, you may also be required to get a flood insurance policy. Be aware that obtaining insurance is mandatory when you first take out a mortgage. Lending institutions want protection on the money they lend you in case there is a loss. In fact, insurance policies include the name of the lending institutions as beneficiaries of the insurance proceeds.

In addition, you are allowed to deduct *Private Mortgage Insurance* (PMI). PMI is generally charged to homeowners who put less than 20% down on the property. It protects the lender by bridging the gap between what the home is worth and what you owe in case you foreclose on the property.

Deduct these types of insurance expenses in the year paid on line 9 of IRS Schedule E.

Legal and Other Professional Fees

In the course of owning your rental property, you may need to seek legal or professional services. Deduct these types of expenses on line 10 of Schedule E. Use this line to deduct legal expenses incurred for evicting a tenant, tax preparation fees relating to the rental property, the cost of this book, and any legal or tax advice regarding the property.

Management Fees

Very busy landlords or landlords who live abroad may find it necessary to employ a company to manage their real estate property. These companies are directly responsible for the operations of the rental property, including the collection of rent. These companies usually give you a monthly accounting of the rental activities such as the rent collected, the expenses incurred, and the management fees. Deduct the management fees you paid to these companies on line 11 of Schedule E. Most rental property owners try to optimize profit by managing their own properties, so the use of a management company is rare.

Mortgage Interest Paid to Banks

On line 12 of Schedule E, deduct the interest reported on your year-end bank statement Form 1098. Remember to wait for all the bank statements before entering this amount on line 12. It is common to have your mortgage loan sold several times to different lending institutions. Therefore, if the loan is sold in the course of the year, you will receive a Form 1098 from each bank the mortgage payments were made to. If you have two mortgages or home equity loans, add all the interest together and enter the total amount on line 12.

Other Interest

If you make loan payments to an individual or company that is not a financial institution (a very rare occurrence), enter the amount of interest paid on line 13 of Schedule E. These private loan arrangements generally do not report interest to the IRS; therefore, Form 1098 is never issued. These arrangements are complicated, so if you fall into this category it is best to let an accountant figure out the amount of interest you can deduct each year.

Repairs

Only deduct repairs when paid on line 14 of Schedule E. A repair is an expense paid to keep the rental property in working condition and adds no significant value to the property. Do not confuse repairs with improvements. For a detailed discussion on how to distinguish between a repair and an improvement, see page 20. Improvements have to be depreciated and deducted on line 20 of Schedule E as discussed later on in this chapter on page 84.

Supplies

You will be going to the store to buy many supplies for the rental property. You are going to need garbage bags, recycling bins, salt for the snow, cleaning supplies, and so on. Deduct these expenses on line 15 of Schedule E.

Taxes

Deduct annual real estate taxes assessed on the rental, such as town and school taxes, on line 16 of Schedule E. If you have a mortgage, property taxes paid during the year are usually reported on the year-end Form 1098 statement.

Utilities

Line 17 of Schedule E is a line that is frequently used. Enter all utility expenses when they are paid, including oil or natural gas used to heat the home. Also include the electricity needed to run the boiler, light up common areas, and so on. You can even deduct ordinary and necessary telephone expenses that relate to the rental activities.

Other

Expenses that are not mentioned above or below should be listed by category on line 18 of Schedule E. These expenses should be ordinary and necessary, and the expense should be for services or items that have a usefulness of less than one year. Therefore, the expense should not be for something that adds significant value to the property. Items or services that add significant value to the property or have a usefulness of more than one year should be depreciated as discussed in the next section.

Helpful Hint:

You cannot deduct loss of rental income during the time a tenant refuses to pay rent or for the time the property was vacant. The loss is automatically reflected because you still will be deducting rental expenses while reporting no income for this period.

Depreciation Expenses

In Chapter 5 you learned how to depreciate the purchase price and closing cost of rental property. In addition, there are going to be many other depreciable expenses, such as improvements, appliances, furnishing, and other items that have a usefulness of more than one year. The table below is a general list of depreciable items and related recovery periods that are commonly used in rental property.

General List of Depreciable Items

Type of Expense	Recovery Period
Appliances, stove, and refrigerator	5 Years
Carpeting	5 Years
Furniture used in rentals	5 Years
Office computers, typewriters, and copiers	5 Years
Office furniture, desks, and file cabinets	7 Years
Sidewalks, shrubbery, and fencing	15 Years
Improvements	27½ Years
Purchase price	27½ Years

As you can see, depreciable expenses are high-ticket items and usually cost a lot of money. The IRS controls how you deduct these expenses through depreciation. You should not be concerned about how to determine the amount that has to be deducted each year for these types of expenses. A reputable software program can easily calculate the deduction. What is important is to understand that these types of items must be deducted over time through depreciation.

Use line 20 of IRS Schedule E to deduct the total amount of depreciable expenses. In addition, in the first year that you purchase a depreciable item you will have to report it on IRS Form 4562 (this is only necessary in the first year). You also must keep good records listing all your depreciable items and the amount of depreciation taken each year for each of these items. It cannot be stressed enough how any reputable tax software can make the depreciation process easy and also assist you in maintaining the depreciation records and reports you will need for the future.

Rental Loss

The IRS views rental activities as a passive type of activity. Unlike professions such as medicine, real estate sales, or electrical contracting, owning rental property does not consume most of your time, nor do you rely on its income to sustain your lifestyles. Therefore, the IRS has put limits on the amount of loss you can deduct from your combined passive activities.

In most cases, in the first few years of purchasing rental property you will operate at a loss. However, the IRS will only allow you to deduct up to $25,000 a year in combined rental losses as long as you actively participate in the rental activity and do not earn over a certain amount of income.

Active Participation

The good news is that *active participation* is an easy test to pass. The IRS says if you own at least 10% of the rental property and make certain management decisions such as setting the rental terms, approving tenants, or other similar decisions, then you actively participated in the rental activity. That is simple enough.

Passive Activity Limitations

The bad news is that if your gross income with certain adjustments is over $150,000, then you cannot deduct any rental activity losses. The loss deduction also phases out between $100,000 and $150,000 (the loss is reduced by 50% of each dollar above $100,000). It is not clear why the IRS would penalize taxpayers who earn a couple of dollars and invest them in rental property. Why wouldn't these individuals be given the same type of tax relief as people who earn under $100,000? Nevertheless, rules are rules, and you must abide by them.

One good thing about this rule is that the IRS allows you to carry over any loss to future years until it is used up. Therefore, once your rental property starts to operate out of the red you will be able to offset any profit with any past carry-over losses. Form 8582 is used to keep track of this madness. Again, if you use any reputable tax software, it will look at your income and generate any necessary supplemental schedule like Form 8582. You should just be aware of the limitations.

Rules for Condominiums and Cooperatives

The IRS treats condominiums in the same fashion as any rental residential home. The difference between a condominium and a residential rental home is that assessment fees have to be collected from the condominium owners to pay for the upkeep of common areas. Unlike a condominium owned for personal use, assessment fees are deductible if the condominium is used for rental purposes. Therefore, in addition to deducting mortgage interest, property taxes, repairs, and depreciation, you should deduct assessment fees in the year paid on Schedule E.

Do not confuse regular assessment fees paid for the upkeep of common areas with special assessments paid for improvements. By now you should know the difference between an improvement and a repair, and you should also be aware that an improvement must be depreciated. With that said, depreciate special assessments for the cost of improvements made to common areas.

That is all there is, and there is nothing more you need to know about renting a condominium. It is that simple.

Renting a Cooperative

Unfortunately, renting out a cooperative apartment is not just like renting out a residential home or condominium. Do not fret—you can use the knowledge you have already gathered in reading this book to understand why the IRS treats certain aspects of cooperative apartments differently from residential rental homes.

Deducting the Cost of the Cooperative Apartment

As explained on page 25, when you own a cooperative apartment you actually own stock certificates in a corporation, which in turn owns all the apartments. Cooperative apartments are unlike residential rental homes or condominiums where the owners actually own the unit they purchased. If you do not own the unit, but only stock certificates, you may wonder how to depreciate the cost of the cooperative apartment, especially knowing that the IRS forces taxpayers to depreciate the purchase price of rental properties.

The amount you are supposed to depreciate is a complex calculation that factors in many variables like the total amount of outstanding shares, mortgage debt on the property, depreciation, and so on. Much of this information cannot be easily obtained by the tenant-stockholder (you). The best way to find out the amount of depreciation on your stock is to ask the accountants who are responsible for the books of the corporation. You should be aware that the depreciation amount provided by the accountants cannot be more than your adjusted cost of the stock when the stock was first purchased. If the accountant's amount is greater, then use the adjusted cost of the stock to depreciate.

Other Deductions for a Cooperative Apartment

Report all the other deductions for the co-op—including mortgage interest, repairs on the apartment, utilities, and depreciation on appliances—as you would if your property was a residential rental property. Also do not forget to deduct all of your maintenance fees, including the part used for the upkeep and repair of common areas. Report all of these deductions on Schedule E.

Similar to condominiums, do not include deductions for payments made in connection with the improvement to common areas. For example, you are not allowed to deduct the reconstruction of the parking garage or the installation of a building-wide alarm system. These expenses must be added to your costs (in this case, the adjusted cost of the stock).

Comprehensive Illustration

Ann, who earns $85,000 a year as a nurse in a hospital, decided to purchase a rental property on February 1, 2007. The property cost $250,000, of which $200,000 related to the building and $50,000 was for the land. The property was ready and available for rent on the day she closed. In addition, the closing costs for the abstract fees, legal fees, title insurance, and transfer taxes were $13,500.

During 2007 Ann collected $10,500 in rental income and incurred the following expenses.

Cleaning	$ 311	Hazard Insurance	$ 1,011
PMI	$ 929	Interest	$12,256
Repairs	$ 731	Replace Balcony	$ 7,000
Property Tax	$ 2,261	Refrigerator	$ 568
Natural Gas	$ 407	*The First Time*	
Exterminator	$ 225	*Homeowner's Tax*	
		Guide	$ 14

As can be seen in Illustration 6.1, Ann reports the rental income and ordinary expenses on Schedule E. The total depreciation on line 20 for the purchase price, closing costs, balcony, and refrigerator is summarized on IRS Form 4562. Lastly, the rental loss of $14,733 shown on line 23 of Schedule E is transferred to Line 17 of Form 1040. Ann's rental loss is not limited and therefore she is able to offset total rental loss against her nurse wages.

ILLUSTRATION 6.1

Form **1040**   **U.S. Individual Income Tax Return**

For the year Jan 1 - Dec 31,   , or other tax year beginning   , ending   , 20

Label (See instructions.)

Use the IRS label. Otherwise, please print or type.

Your first name: Ann   MI   Last name

If a joint return, spouse's first name   MI   Last name

Home address (number and street). If you have a P.O. box, see instructions.   Apartment no.
107 Strawberry Street

City, town or post office. If you have a foreign address, see instructions.   State   ZIP code
Los Angeles   CA   99391

Last name: Clarke

Your social security number: 123-45-6789

Spouse's social security number

▲ **Important!** ▲
You **must** enter your social security number(s) above.

Presidential Election Campaign (See instructions.) ▶ Note: Checking 'Yes' will not change your tax or reduce your refund.
Do you, or your spouse if filing a joint return, want $3 to go to this fund? . . . . ▶
You: Yes [ ] No [ ]   Spouse: Yes [ ] No [ ]

Filing Status
Check only one box.

1 [X] Single
2 [ ] Married filing jointly (even if only one had income)
3 [ ] Married filing separately. Enter spouse's SSN above & full name here. ▶
4 [ ] Head of household (with qualifying person). (See instructions.) If the qualifying person is a child but not your dependent, enter this child's name here ▶
5 [ ] Qualifying widow(er) with dependent child (see instructions)

Exemptions

6a [X] Yourself. If someone can claim you as a dependent, **do not** check box 6a. . . . .
b [ ] Spouse . . . .

c Dependents:
(1) First name   Last name
(2) Dependent's social security number
(3) Dependent's relationship to you
(4) ✓ if qualifying child for child tax credit (see instrs)

Boxes checked on 6a and 6b: 1
No. of children on 6c who:
● lived with you . . .
● did not live with you due to divorce or separation (see instrs) . .
Dependents on 6c not entered above .

If more than four dependents, see instructions.

d Total number of exemptions claimed . . . .
Add numbers on lines above . . . ▶ 1

Income

Attach Form(s) W-2 here. Also attach Forms W-2G and 1099-R if tax was withheld.

If you did not get a W-2, see instructions.

Enclose, but do not attach, any payment. Also, please use Form 1040-V.

7 Wages, salaries, tips, etc. Attach Form(s) W-2 . . . . | 7 | 85,000.
8a Taxable interest. Attach Schedule B if required . . . . | 8a |
b Tax-exempt interest. **Do not** include on line 8a . . . . | 8b |
9a Ordinary dividends. Attach Schedule B if required . . . . | 9a |
b Qualifd divs (see instrs) . . . . | 9b |
10 Taxable refunds, credits, or offsets of state and local income taxes (see instructions) . . . . | 10 |
11 Alimony received . . . . | 11 |
12 Business income or (loss). Attach Schedule C or C-EZ . . . . . . | 12 |
13 Capital gain or (loss). Att Sch D if reqd. If not reqd, ck here . . . . . . ▶ [ ] | 13 |
14 Other gains or (losses). Attach Form 4797 . . . . | 14 |
15a IRA distributions . . . . . . | 15a | b Taxable amount (see instrs) . . | 15b |
16a Pensions and annuities . . . | 16a | b Taxable amount (see instrs) . . | 16b |
17 Rental real estate, royalties, partnerships, S corporations, trusts, etc. Attach Schedule E . . . | 17 | -14,732.
18 Farm income or (loss). Attach Schedule F . . . . | 18 |
19 Unemployment compensation . . . . | 19 |
20a Social security benefits . . . . . | 20a | b Taxable amount (see instrs) . . | 20b |
21 Other income . . . . | 21 |
22 Add the amounts in the far right column for lines 7 through 21. This is your **total income** . . ▶ | 22 | 70,268.

Adjusted Gross Income

23 Educator expenses (see instructions) . . . . | 23 |
24 Certain business expenses of reservists, performing artists, and fee-basis government officials. Attach Form 2106 or 2106-EZ . . . . | 24 |
25 IRA deduction (see instructions) . . . . | 25 |
26 Student loan interest deduction (see instructions) . . . . | 26 |
27 Tuition and fees deduction (see instructions) . . . . | 27 |
28 Health savings account deduction. Attach Form 8889 . . . . . | 28 |
29 Moving expenses. Attach Form 3903 . . . . | 29 |
30 One-half of self-employment tax. Attach Schedule SE . . . . . | 30 |
31 Self-employed health insurance deduction (see instrs) . . . . | 31 |
32 Self-employed SEP, SIMPLE, and qualified plans . . . . | 32 |
33 Penalty on early withdrawal of savings . . . . | 33 |
34a Alimony paid b Recipient's SSN. . . ▶ _____ . . | 34a |
35 Add lines 23 through 34a . . . . | 35 |
36 Subtract line 35 from line 22. This is your **adjusted gross income** . . . . ▶ | 36 | 70,268.

Transfer from Schedule E

Form 1040

ILLUSTRATION 6.1

Form **1040**	Ann Clarke	123-45-6789	Page **2**

Tax and Credits

37	Amount from line 36 (adjusted gross income)	37	70,268.

38a Check if: ☐ **You** were born before January 2, 1940, ☐ Blind. **Total boxes**
☐ **Spouse** was born before January 2, 1940, ☐ Blind. **checked ▶ 38a** ☐

Standard Deduction for –
• People who checked any box on line 38a or 38b **or** who can be claimed as a dependent, see instructions.

• All others:

Single or Married filing separately, $4,850

Married filing jointly or Qualifying widow(er), $9,700

Head of household, $7,150

b	If your spouse itemizes on a separate return, or you were a dual-status alien, see instructions and check here . . . . ▶ 38b ☐		
39	**Itemized deductions** (from Schedule A) or your **standard deduction** (see left margin)	39	7,000.
40	Subtract line 39 from line 37	40	63,268.
41	If line 37 is $107,025 or less, multiply $3,100 by the total number of exemptions claimed on line 6d. If line 37 is over $107,025, see the worksheet in the instructions	41	3,100.
42	**Taxable income.** Subtract line 41 from line 40. If line 41 is more than line 40, enter -0-	42	60,168.
43	**Tax** (see instrs). Check if any tax is from: **a** ☐ Form(s) 8814 **b** ☐ Form 4972	43	11,781.
44	**Alternative minimum tax** (see instructions). Attach Form 6251	44	0.
45	Add lines 43 and 44 . . . . ▶	45	11,781.

46	Foreign tax credit. Attach Form 1116 if required	46	
47	Credit for child and dependent care expenses. Attach Form 2441	47	
48	Credit for the elderly or the disabled. Attach Schedule R	48	
49	Education credits. Attach Form 8863	49	
50	Retirement savings contributions credit. Attach Form 8880 . . .	50	
51	Child tax credit (see instructions).	51	
52	Adoption credit. Attach Form 8839	52	
53	Credits from: **a** ☐ Form 8396 **b** ☐ Form 8859	53	
54	Other credits. Check applicable box(es): **a** ☐ Form 3800 **b** ☐ Form 8801 **c** ☐ Specify_____	54	

55	Add lines 46 through 54. These are your **total credits**	55	
56	Subtract line 55 from line 45. If line 55 is more than line 45, enter -0- . . . . ▶	56	11,781.

Other Taxes

57	Self-employment tax. Attach Schedule SE	57	
58	Social security and Medicare tax on tip income not reported to employer. Attach Form 4137	58	
59	Additional tax on IRAs, other qualified retirement plans, etc. Attach Form 5329 if required	59	
60	Advance earned income credit payments from Form(s) W-2	60	
61	Household employment taxes. Attach Schedule H	61	
62	Add lines 56-61. This is your **total tax** . . . . ▶	62	11,781.

Payments

If you have a qualifying child, attach Schedule EIC.

63	Federal income tax withheld from Forms W-2 and 1099	63	15,335.
64	2004 estimated tax payments and amount applied from 2003 return	64	
65a	**Earned income credit (EIC).** . . . . No	65a	
b	Nontaxable combat pay election . . . ▶	65b	
66	Excess social security and tier 1 RRTA tax withheld (see instructions) . . .	66	
67	Additional child tax credit. Attach Form 8812	67	
68	Amount paid with request for extension to file (see instructions)	68	
69	Other pmts from: **a** ☐ Form 2439 **b** ☐ Form 4136 **c** ☐ Form 8885	69	
70	Add lines 63, 64, 65a, and 66 through 69. These are your **total payments** . . . . ▶	70	15,335.

Refund

Direct deposit? See instructions and fill in 72b, 72c, and 72d.

71	If line 70 is more than line 62, subtract line 62 from line 70. This is the amount you **overpaid**	71	3,554.
72a	Amount of line 71 you want **refunded to you** . . . . ▶	72a	3,554.
▶ b	Routing number . . . . . XXXXXXXXX ▶ **c** Type: ☐ Checking ☐ Savings		
▶ d	Account number XXXXXXXXXXXXXXXXX		
73	Amount of line 71 you want **applied to your 2005 estimated tax** . . . . ▶	73	

Amount You Owe

74	**Amount you owe.** Subtract line 70 from line 62. For details on how to pay, see instructions . . . . ▶	74	
75	Estimated tax penalty (see instructions)	75	

Third Party Designee

Do you want to allow another person to discuss this return with the IRS (see instructions)? . . . . . . ☐ **Yes.** Complete the following. ☒ **No**

Designee's name ▶	Phone no. ▶	Personal identification number (PIN) ▶

Sign Here
Joint return? See instructions.
Keep a copy for your records.

Under penalties of perjury, I declare that I have examined this return and accompanying schedules and statements, and to the best of my knowledge and belief, they are true, correct, and complete. Declaration of preparer (other than taxpayer) is based on all information of which preparer has any knowledge.

Your signature ▶	Date	Your occupation Nurse	Daytime phone number
Spouse's signature. If a joint return, **both** must sign. ▶	Date	Spouse's occupation	

Paid Preparer's Use Only

Self-Prepared

Preparer's signature ▶	Date	Check if self-employed ☐	Preparer's SSN or PTIN
Firm's name (or yours if self-employed), ▶ address, and ZIP code		EIN Phone no.	

Form **1040**

ILLUSTRATION 6.1

SCHEDULE E (Form 1040)	Supplemental Income and Loss (From rental real estate, royalties, partnerships, S corporations, estates, trusts, REMICs, etc) ► Attach to Form 1040 or Form 1041. ► See Instructions for Schedule E (Form 1040).	

Name(s) shown on return	Your social security number
Ann Clarke	123-45-6789

Part I　Income or Loss From Rental Real Estate and Royalties　Note. If you are in the business of renting personal property, use **Schedule C** or **C-EZ** (see instructions). Report farm rental income or loss from **Form 4835** on page 2, line 40.

1	List the type and location of each **rental real estate property:**		2	For each rental real estate property listed on line 1, did you or your family use it during the tax year for personal purposes for more than the greater of: ● 14 days, or ● 10% of the total days rented at fair rental value? (See instructions.)		Yes	No
A	One Family Home 2 Western St, Los Angeles CA				A		X
B					B		
C					C		

Income:		Properties			Totals
		A	B	C	(Add columns A, B, and C.)
3	Rents received	**3**	10,500.			**3**	10,500.
4	Royalties received	**4**				**4**	
Expenses:						
5	Advertising	**5**				
6	Auto and travel (see instructions)	**6**				
7	Cleaning and maintenance	**7**	311.			
8	Commissions.	**8**				
9	Insurance	**9**	1,940.			
10	Legal and other professional fees. . . .	**10**	14.			
11	Management fees	**11**				
12	Mortgage interest paid to banks, etc (see instructions)	**12**	12,256.			**12**	12,256.
13	Other interest.	**13**				
14	Repairs.	**14**	731.			
15	Supplies	**15**				
16	Taxes	**16**	2,261.			
17	Utilities	**17**	407.			
18	Other (list) ► Exterminator		225.			
		18				
19	Add lines 5 through 18	**19**	18,145.			**19**	18,145.
20	Depreciation expense or depletion (see instructions)	**20**	7,087.			**20**	7,087.
21	Total expenses. Add lines 19 and 20 . .	**21**	25,232.			
22	Income or (loss) from rental real estate or royalty properties. Subtract line 21 from line 3 (rents) or line 4 (royalties). If the result is a (loss), see instructions to find out if you must file **Form 6198**	**22**	-14,732.			
23	Deductible rental real estate loss. **Caution.** Your rental real estate loss on line 22 may be limited. See instructions to find out if you must file **Form 8582**. Real estate professionals must complete line 43 on page 2	**23**	-14,732.			
24	**Income.** Add positive amounts shown on line 22. **Do not** include any losses					**24**	
25	**Losses.** Add royalty losses from line 22 and rental real estate losses from line 23. Enter total losses here					**25**	-14,732.
26	**Total rental real estate and royalty income or (loss).** Combine lines 24 and 25. Enter the result here. If Parts II, III, IV, and line 40 on page 2 do not apply to you, also enter this amount on Form 1040, line 17. Otherwise, include this amount in the total on line 41 on page 2.					**26**	-14,732.

Schedule E (Form 1040)

The part of the gain that has to be taxed as ordinary income depends on the amount of depreciation you have taken on your tax returns throughout the years. You must treat the gain as ordinary income to the extent of the total depreciation deducted (or meant to have been deducted) on your tax returns. The gain in excess of depreciation is taxed at the more favorable capital gain rate.

Example:
Tatiana had a $15,000 gain from the sale of her rental property. She had depreciated a total of $10,000 on her tax returns while she owned the property. Assuming her ordinary tax rate is 20% and her capital tax rate is 10%, then Tatiana will be responsible for paying $2,500 in taxes [($10,000 x .20) +($5,000 x .10)]. The capital gain tax rates for Tatiana were lower and of course more desirable than ordinary income tax rates.

Determining Your Gain or Loss

You should understand the true effects of depreciation and why taking this deduction through the years in reality has never given you a tax break. So far you know that you are able to depreciate the cost of the rental property and those expensive home improvements. What you did not know is that when you sell the property the IRS forces you to reduce the cost of the rental property for all the depreciation you have taken while you owned the property. If you have a gain, this adjustment normally results in paying taxes on some or all of the depreciation you have taken throughout the years. In addition, as discussed on page 102, the amount of taxes you have to pay on this part of the gain is based on the higher ordinary tax rate.

However, before you get upset you should understand why the IRS requires you to reduce the cost for the depreciation taken while you owned the rental property. In the years you depreciated the cost of the property and improvements, you were able to deduct a portion of those costs on line 20 of Schedule E. As a result, you generally got a tax benefit in those years. Now that it is time to sell the home, the IRS says, "Since you got a tax benefit in the years you depreciated the purchase price and improvements, you need to adjust the cost of the rental property by the amount you depreciated. Without this adjustment, you would be getting another tax benefit because you would be determining the gain or loss by using the original cost with no consideration as to what you have already deducted through depreciation."

The motto for depreciation should be "deduct now but pay later." Still, if you do not depreciate, the IRS will make an adjustment for depreciation even if you did not take the deduction, so you should always depreciate your rental property.

You may wonder why you should bother owning a rental property. The primary reason to own rental property should not be to try to save on your taxes. You may be able to deduct now for temporary tax relief only to pay later. The primary reason why you invest in rental property is because real estate has historically gone up in value and as long as the rents can maintain the property expenses, you will eventually pay off the loan and in time your rental property will return back much more than what you paid out. In addition, since real estate is an investment that has historically appreciated in value, you can sell for much more than what you paid.

How to Determine the Gain or Loss

To determine if you have a gain or loss from the sale of your rental property you must know the selling price and the adjusted cost (*basis*) of the property. The difference between the selling price and the adjusted cost is either a gain or loss from the sale of the rental property.

Sales Price

The sales price is simply the amount of money for which you sold the rental property. If you do not remember how much you sold the property for, you can easily find the selling price on the sales contract.

Adjusted Cost (Basis)

Determining the adjusted cost of rental property is very similar to determining the cost of a personal home. The difference is that with rental property you have to subtract out the depreciation and add back any selling costs. The formula for calculating the adjusted cost is simple addition and is as follows:

> Purchase Price
>
> \+ Certain Closing Costs
>
> \+ Improvements and other depreciable items
>
> – Depreciation
>
> \+ Selling Costs (such as commissions)
>
> Adjusted Cost

The first thing you need to do is ascertain the purchase price. The *purchase price* is simply the amount you paid for the home and can easily be located on the closing statement (HUD 1) that you received when you first purchased the home.

Second, add to the purchase price certain closing costs you paid when you first bought the rental property. These are the same closing costs that you should have added back to the purchase price and been depreciating all along.

Third, add any improvements and other depreciable items purchased while you owned the rental property. Remember that you should have been keeping good records listing all your depreciable items this whole time. Now you need those records. Look at the list and add to the purchase price and closing fees the costs of improvements and other depreciable items. If you used a reputable tax software, then you should be able to print out a copy of all the depreciable items with a snap of your fingers.

Fourth, subtract the depreciation that you should have taken each year for items that the IRS requires you to deduct over time. Again, you should have good records or a tax program to determine the amount of depreciation that was taken on the property. This is an important adjustment for the IRS because what you deducted in the past must be paid for now. Otherwise you will be getting a double tax benefit. So be very careful that you properly reduce the cost of the property basis by the depreciation that you took (or should have taken) throughout the years.

Lastly, add back in any expenses incurred from the sale of the property. Examples of selling expenses are commissions paid to real estate agents for selling the home and fees charged by your lawyer for processing the sales contract and representing you during the sale.

Once you know the sales price and the adjusted costs, you are ready to calculate whether you have a gain or loss from the sale of your rental property. Simply subtract the adjusted cost from the sales price and the results will be either a gain or a loss.

Example:

Michiko sold her five-family rental property in 2006 for $900,000. The sales price was stated on the sales contract. She purchased the property eight years ago for $450,000, which included certain closing costs of $15,000 that had to be depreciated. Throughout the years Michiko made improvements totaling $125,000. The total depreciation she claimed throughout the years was $75,000. The costs associated with selling the property amounted to $35,000. Below is the calculation of Michiko's gain from the sale of her rental property.

Sales Price		$ 900,000

Adjusted Cost:		
Purchase Price	+ $435,000	
Closing Costs	+ 15,000	
Improvements	+ 125,000	
Depreciation	− 75,000	
Selling Costs	+ 35,000	535,000
Gain		$ 365,000

Helpful Hint

Often, individuals who sell their rental property are in shock when they find themselves facing a substantial gain although they received little or no money from the sale. It is not hard to understand why this has happened. One reason this happens is depreciation. For example, if you sold a rental property for the same price that you bought it for ten years ago, then at minimum you will have a gain based on the total amount of depreciation you deducted on your tax returns while you owned the property.

Another reason for having a large gain with little return when the property is sold is that individuals borrow against the equity on the properties. Therefore, if you take out additional mortgages or equity loans while owning the property, you are in a sense cashing out on your investment. If you take out too much with no regard to the tax ramifications at the time of the sale, you may find yourself owing more in taxes than what you receive from the sale. Be careful.

Calculating the Tax

You must determine the part of the gain that will be taxed at your ordinary income tax rate and the part that will be taxed at the lower capital gain rates. The IRS requires you to tax the gain as ordinary income to the extent of depreciation deducted (or should have been deducted) and any excess gain should be taxed at the lower capital gain rates. In Michiko's case, she would have to pay taxes as ordinary income on the first $75,000 and capital gain taxes on the remaining $290,000 ($365,000 – $75,000).

To put this discussion in further perspective, look at how the ordinary tax rates differ from capital tax rates. If Michiko's ordinary tax rate is 25% and her capital tax rate is 15%, then she will be paying the lower 15% tax rate on the $290,000. Anyone in their right mind would rather pay taxes on the lower rate.

The tax rates on capital gains have been changing dynamically during the last few years. In comparison to the past, these changes have resulted in low tax rates. For example, the capital gain rate in 2006 was:

- 5% if the taxpayer's tax bracket was 15% or less, or
- 15% if the taxpayer's tax bracket was greater than 15%.

Please note that the capital gains laws may change frequently. Therefore, check IRS Publication 17 at **www.irs.gov** or with your accountant to get the latest information on the capital gain rates.

Keeping Records

Selling your rental property can be a very stressful event. Not only do you have to worry about whether you have to pay taxes on the sale, you also have to gather all the necessary records to determine whether there is a gain or loss from the sale. To reduce some of the stress, it is important that you maintain proper records while you own the rental property. These records should include all the original closing documents, yearly worksheets of the rental income and expenses, receipts of all the improvements, and depreciation records.

Reporting the Sale of Rental Property

Unlike the sale of a personal residence, regardless of whether there is a gain or loss from the sale of rental property you must report the sale to the IRS, since the IRS views owning rental property as owning any type of business. It should be no surprise that when you sell rental property you have to use the same form that is generally used to sell business property. Report the sale of rental property on IRS Form 4797. If there is a gain, transfer the information from Form 4797 to Schedule D of your personal tax return. The formulas and worksheets in Schedule D take the gain and charge ordinary income tax rates to the extent of depreciation and capital gain rates on the excess gain.

Although 1) the mechanics of how to determine whether there is a gain or loss and 2) the concept of being charged ordinary tax rates on the gain to the extent of depreciation and capital rates on the excess may be simple, using the IRS form to report the sale may not be as simple. Therefore, considering how significant a transaction selling rental property is, you are strongly encouraged to have the return done by a qualified tax preparer. Still, even if you use such an individual you must provide him or her with all the necessary records to report the gain or loss.

If you decide to prepare the taxes yourself, stick with one reputable tax program while you own the property and use the program to report the sale. Also, refer to IRS Publication 544, "Sales and Other Disposition of Assets," for further discussion on reporting the sale of rental property.

Step-by-Step Illustration

Paul, a retired police officer, purchased a four-family rental property in February 2005. The cost of the property was $400,000, which included $375,000 for the building, $15,000 for the land, and $10,000 for depreciable closing costs.

In July 2005, Paul paid contractors $50,000 to perform some well-needed renovations on his rental property. He properly depreciated the costs of the improvement on Schedule E in 2005.

Being a shrewd businessman, Paul bought *The First Time Homeowner's Tax Guide* to educate himself on owning and selling rental property. He kept impeccable records and decided to do his own taxes using reputable tax software. In October 2006, more than one year after he purchased the rental property, he sold it for $570,000, and he paid the real estate agent $30,000 in commission.

During 2006 Paul received $22,000 in pension and earned $25,000 in rental income. He also had the following expenses: mortgage interest of $6,000 and heating oil of $1,500.

Step 1: Gather All the Necessary Documents

You will need the following:

- closing statement or HUD 1 from when you sold the rental property;
- closing statement or HUD 1 from when you first bought the rental property;
- records of all improvements;
- depreciation reports; and,
- IRS Publication 544 (you can download this publication from **www.irs.gov**).

Step 2: Determine the Sales Price

This should be one of the easiest steps. The sales price is simply the sales price that is listed on the HUD 1 or sales contract. That is it! Paul sold his rental property for $570,000.

Step 3: Determine the Adjusted Cost

Using the HUD 1 that was issued when the rental property was first bought and the depreciation reports, Paul determines the adjusted cost.

$ 390,000	Purchase Price (Building and Land)
+ 10,000	(Depreciable Closing Costs)
+ 50,000	(Improvements and other depreciable items)
- 25,605	(Depreciation)
+ 30,000	(Selling Costs (e.g., commissions))
$454,395	(Adjusted Cost)

Step 4: Determine the Gain or Loss

This is another very simple step; just subtract Step 3 from Step 2.

	Amount	Taken From:
Sales Price	$ 570,000	Step 2
Adjusted Cost	- $ 454,395	Step 3
GAIN	$115,605	

Paul has a substantial gain and of course will have to pay taxes. Now to put everything into perspective, apply the IRS's rules on how to tax the gain from the sale of rental property. The IRS requires you to tax the gain as ordinary income to the extent of depreciation deducted, and any excess gain should be taxed at the lower capital gain rates.

Therefore, Paul would be paying taxes on the first $25,605 based on the ordinary income tax rates. The tax on the excess gain of $90,000 is based on the more favorable capital tax gain rates. Now comes the less simple part—reporting the sale on the IRS's not-so-simple tax forms.

Step 5: Report the Taxable Gain

Before you can report the gain or loss, you must first assign the total sales price to the building, the land, and each item that was depreciated while you owned the property. Since the total cost of the rental property is made up of many amounts, you have to assign to each amount the related sales price, because the IRS wants you to report the land transaction on one part of IRS Form 4797 and the building and other depreciable items on another part of the form. It is unclear why the IRS makes this so difficult.

Another problem is that the IRS gives you little to no direction on how to assign the amounts to the separate costs that make up the rental property. They only say to use the fair market value of the land and building to assign the sales price. The problem with that limited advice is what to do with all the depreciable items (improvements and appliances) that you acquired at various times, which all make up the cost of the rental property.

Whatever method you use to assign the price, make sure that you at least try first to properly assign the land cost. For all other depreciable items, try to assign an amount equal to or greater than the original cost. This should not be a problem if there is a gain. This may be a problem if there is a loss.

In Paul's case, he properly assigned the land a value of $45,000, which he got from the tax assessment values. Then he arbitrarily assigned $50,000 to the improvement and the remaining $475,000 to the building ($570,000 – $95,000). He assigned $50,000 because this amount is what he paid for the improvement, and most importantly, the amount is equal to the original cost.

Review Illustration 7.1 to understand how Paul's rental property was reported. As you can see, the gain reported on IRS Form 4797 was transferred over to Schedule D. Schedule D will take the gain and charge ordinary income tax rates to the extent of depreciation and capital gain rates on the excess gain. You will notice that Paul will be paying taxes on the first $25,605 based on the ordinary income tax rates and pay capital gain rates on the excess gain of $90,000.

ILLUSTRATION 7.1

Form **1040**	U.S. Individual Income Tax Return		

For the year Jan 1 - Dec 31,   , or other tax year beginning   , ending   , 20

Label (See instructions.)

Your first name   MI   Last name

Paul   Myers

Your social security number

123-45-6789

If a joint return, spouse's first name   MI   Last name

Spouse's social security number

Use the IRS label. Otherwise, please print or type.

Home address (number and street). If you have a P.O. box, see instructions.   Apartment no.

307 Snake Road

▲ **Important!** ▲
You **must** enter your social security number(s) above.

City, town or post office. If you have a foreign address, see instructions.   State   ZIP code

Houston   TX   99999

Presidential Election Campaign (See instructions.)

Note: Checking 'Yes' will not change your tax or reduce your refund.

▶ Do you, or your spouse if filing a joint return, want $3 to go to this fund? . . . . ▶

You: Yes ☐ No ☐   Spouse: Yes ☐ No ☐

Filing Status

Check only one box.

1 ☒ Single
2 ☐ Married filing jointly (even if only one had income)
3 ☐ Married filing separately. Enter spouse's SSN above & full name here. ▶
4 ☐ Head of household (with qualifying person). (See instructions.) If the qualifying person is a child but not your dependent, enter this child's name here. ▶
5 ☐ Qualifying widow(er) with dependent child (see instructions)

Exemptions

6a ☒ **Yourself.** If someone can claim you as a dependent, **do not** check box 6a. . . . .
b ☐ **Spouse** . . . .

Boxes checked on 6a and 6b . 1

c **Dependents:**

(1) First name Last name	(2) Dependent's social security number	(3) Dependent's relationship to you	(4) ✓ if qualifying child for child tax credit (see instrs)

No. of children on 6c who:
• lived with you . . .
• did not live with you due to divorce or separation (see instrs) . .
Dependents on 6c not entered above .

If more than four dependents, see instructions.

d Total number of exemptions claimed . . . .

Add numbers on lines above . . . ▶ 1

Income

Attach Form(s) W-2 here. Also attach Forms W-2G and 1099-R if tax was withheld.

If you did not get a W-2, see instructions.

Enclose, but do not attach, any payment. Also, please use Form 1040-V.

7	Wages, salaries, tips, etc. Attach Form(s) W-2	7	
8a	Taxable interest. Attach Schedule B if required	8a	
b	Tax-exempt interest. **Do not** include on line 8a 8b		
9a	Ordinary dividends. Attach Schedule B if required	9a	
b	Qualtd divs (see instrs) 9b		
10	Taxable refunds, credits, or offsets of state and local income taxes (see instructions)	10	
11	Alimony received.	11	
12	Business income or (loss). Attach Schedule C or C-EZ	12	
13	Capital gain or (loss). Att Sch D if reqd. If not reqd, ck here . . . . ▶ ☐	13	115,605.
14	Other gains or (losses). Attach Form 4797	14	
15a	IRA distributions . . . . . . 15a b Taxable amount (see instrs) . .	15b	
16a	Pensions and annuities . . . 16a b Taxable amount (see instrs) . .	16b	22,000.
17	Rental real estate, royalties, partnerships, S corporations, trusts, etc. Attach Schedule E . . .	17	4,978.
18	Farm income or (loss). Attach Schedule F	18	
19	Unemployment compensation	19	
20a	Social security benefits . . . . . . 20a b Taxable amount (see instrs) . .	20b	
21	Other income	21	
22	Add the amounts in the far right column for lines 7 through 21. This is your **total income** . . ▶	22	142,583.

Transfer from Schedule D

Adjusted Gross Income

23	Educator expenses (see instructions)	23	
24	Certain business expenses of reservists, performing artists, and fee-basis government officials. Attach Form 2106 or 2106-EZ	24	
25	IRA deduction (see instructions)	25	
26	Student loan interest deduction (see instructions)	26	
27	Tuition and fees deduction (see instructions)	27	
28	Health savings account deduction. Attach Form 8889	28	
29	Moving expenses. Attach Form 3903.	29	
30	One-half of self-employment tax. Attach Schedule SE	30	
31	Self-employed health insurance deduction (see instrs)	31	
32	Self-employed SEP, SIMPLE, and qualified plans	32	
33	Penalty on early withdrawal of savings	33	
34a	Alimony paid b Recipient's SSN . . . ▶	34a	
35	Add lines 23 through 34a	35	
36	Subtract line 35 from line 22. This is your **adjusted gross income** . . . . ▶	36	142,583.

Form **1040**

ILLUSTRATION 7.1

Form 1040	Paul Myers					123-45-6789	Page 2

Tax and Credits

37	Amount from line 36 (adjusted gross income)	37	142,583.

38a Check if: ☐ **You** were born before January 2, 1940, ☐ Blind. ☐ **Spouse** was born before January 2, 1940, ☐ Blind. **Total boxes checked ►** 38a

b If your spouse itemizes on a separate return, or you were a dual-status alien, see instructions and check here ► 38b ☐

Standard Deduction for –
- People who checked any box on line 38a or 38b or who can be claimed as a dependent, see instructions.
- All others:

Single or Married filing separately, $4,850

Married filing jointly or Qualifying widow(er), $9,700

Head of household, $7,150

39	**Itemized deductions** (from Schedule A) or your **standard deduction** (see left margin)	39	4,850.
40	Subtract line 39 from line 37	40	137,733.
41	If line 37 is $107,025 or less, multiply $3,100 by the total number of exemptions claimed on line 6d. If line 37 is over $107,025, see the worksheet in the instructions	41	3,100.
42	**Taxable income.** Subtract line 41 from line 40. If line 41 is more than line 40, enter -0-	42	134,633.
43	**Tax** (see instrs). Check if any tax is from: a ☐ Form(s) 8814 b ☐ Form 4972	43	21,402.
44	**Alternative minimum tax** (see instructions). Attach Form 6251	44	
45	Add lines 43 and 44 ►	45	21,402.
46	Foreign tax credit. Attach Form 1116 if required 46		
47	Credit for child and dependent care expenses. Attach Form 2441 47		
48	Credit for the elderly or the disabled. Attach Schedule R 48		
49	Education credits. Attach Form 8863 49		
50	Retirement savings contributions credit. Attach Form 8880 .. 50		
51	Child tax credit (see instructions) 51		
52	Adoption credit. Attach Form 8839 52		
53	Credits from: a ☐ Form 8396 b ☐ Form 8859 .. 53		
54	Other credits. Check applicable box(es): a ☐ Form 3800 b ☐ Form 8801 c ☐ Specify _____ 54		
55	Add lines 46 through 54. These are your **total credits**	55	
56	Subtract line 55 from line 45. If line 55 is more than line 45, enter -0- ►	56	21,402.

Other Taxes

57	Self-employment tax. Attach Schedule SE	57	
58	Social security and Medicare tax on tip income not reported to employer. Attach Form 4137	58	
59	Additional tax on IRAs, other qualified retirement plans, etc. Attach Form 5329 if required	59	
60	Advance earned income credit payments from Form(s) W-2	60	
61	Household employment taxes. Attach Schedule H	61	
62	Add lines 56-61. This is your **total tax** ►	62	21,402.

Payments

If you have a qualifying child, attach Schedule EIC.

63	Federal income tax withheld from Forms W-2 and 1099 63		
64	2004 estimated tax payments and amount applied from 2003 return 64		
65a	**Earned income credit (EIC).** 65a		
b	Nontaxable combat pay election .. ► 65b		
66	Excess social security and tier 1 RRTA tax withheld (see instructions) ... 66		
67	Additional child tax credit. Attach Form 8812 67		
68	Amount paid with request for extension to file (see instructions) 68		
69	Other pmts from: a ☐ Form 2439 b ☐ Form 4136 c ☐ Form 8885 69		
70	Add lines 63, 64, 65a, and 66 through 69. These are your **total payments** ►	70	

Refund

Direct deposit? See instructions and fill in 72b, 72c, and 72d.

71	If line 70 is more than line 62, subtract line 62 from line 70. This is the amount you **overpaid**	71	
72a	Amount of line 71 you want **refunded to you** ►	72a	
► b	Routing number ..... ► c Type: ☐ Checking ☐ Savings		
► d	Account number		
73	Amount of line 71 you want **applied to your 2005 estimated tax** .... ► 73		

Amount You Owe

74	**Amount you owe.** Subtract line 70 from line 62. For details on how to pay, see instructions ...... ►	74	21,402.
75	Estimated tax penalty (see instructions) 75		

Third Party Designee

Do you want to allow another person to discuss this return with the IRS (see instructions)? ..... ☐ **Yes. Complete the following.** ☒ No

Designee's name ►   Phone no. ►   Personal identification number (PIN) ►

Sign Here

Joint return? See instructions.

Keep a copy for your records.

Under penalties of perjury, I declare that I have examined this return and accompanying schedules and statements, and to the best of my knowledge and belief, they are true, correct, and complete. Declaration of preparer (other than taxpayer) is based on all information of which preparer has any knowledge.

Your signature   Date   Your occupation   Daytime phone number

Retired

Spouse's signature. If a joint return, **both** must sign.   Date   Spouse's occupation

Paid Preparer's Use Only

Preparer's signature ►   Self-Prepared   Date   Check if self-employed ☐   Preparer's SSN or PTIN

Firm's name (or yours if self-employed), address, and ZIP code   EIN   Phone no.

Form **1040**

ILLUSTRATION 7.1

SCHEDULE D (Form 1040)	Capital Gains and Losses			
	▸ Attach to Form 1040. ▸ See Instructions for Schedule D (Form 1040). ▸ Use Schedule D-1 to list additional transactions for lines 1 and 8.			

Name(s) shown on Form 1040

Paul Myers

Your social security number: 123-45-6789

Part I   Short-Term Capital Gains and Losses — Assets Held One Year or Less

	(a) Description of property (Example: 100 shares XYZ Co)	(b) Date acquired (Mo, day, yr)	(c) Date sold (Mo, day, yr)	(d) Sales price (see instructions)	(e) Cost or other basis (see instructions)	(f) Gain or (loss) Subtract (e) from (d)
1						

2 Enter your short-term totals, if any, from Schedule D-1, line 2 . . . . **2**

3 **Total short-term sales price amounts.** Add lines 1 and 2 in column (d) **3**

4 Short-term gain from Form 6252 and short-term gain or (loss) from Forms 4684, 6781, and 8824 . . . . **4**

5 Net short-term gain or (loss) from partnerships, S corporations, estates, and trusts from Schedule(s) K-1 . . . . . **5**

6 Short-term capital loss carryover. Enter the amount, if any, from line 8 of your **Capital Loss Carryover Worksheet** in the instructions **6**

7 **Net short-term capital gain or (loss).** Combine lines 1 through 6 in column (f) **7**

Part II   Long-Term Capital Gains and Losses — Assets Held More Than One Year

	(a) Description of property (Example: 100 shares XYZ Co)	(b) Date acquired (Mo, day, yr)	(c) Date sold (Mo, day, yr)	(d) Sales price (see instructions)	(e) Cost or other basis (see instructions)	(f) Gain or (loss) Subtract (e) from (d)
8						

Transfer to 1040 line 13

9 Enter your long-term totals, if any, from Schedule D-1, line 9 . . . . **9**

10 **Total long-term sales price amounts.** Add lines 8 and 9 in column (d) **10**

11 Gain from Form 4797, Part I; long-term gain from Forms 2439 and 6252; and long-term gain or (loss) from Forms 4684, 6781, and 8824 . . . . **11**   115,605.

12 Net long-term gain or (loss) from partnerships, S corporations, estates, and trusts from Schedule(s) K-1 . . . . . **12**

13 Capital gain distributions. See instrs **13**

14 Long-term capital loss carryover. Enter the amount, if any, from line 13 of your **Capital Loss Carryover Worksheet** in the instructions **14**

15 **Net long-term capital gain or (loss).** Combine lines 8 through 14 in column (f). Then go to Part III on page 2 . . . . **15**   115,605.

Schedule D (Form 1040)

ILLUSTRATION 7.1

Schedule **D** (Form 1040)   Paul Myers   123-45-6789   Page **2**

| Part III | Summary |

16 Combine lines 7 and 15 and enter the result. If line 16 is a loss, skip lines 17 through 20, and go to line 21.
If a gain, enter the gain on Form 1040, line 13, and then go to line 17 below . . . . | **16** | 115,605.

17 Are lines 15 and 16 **both** gains?

☒ **Yes.** Go to line 18.

☐ **No.** Skip lines 18 through 21, and go to line 22.

18 Enter the amount, if any, from line 7 of the **28% Rate Gain Worksheet** in the instructions . . . . ▶ | **18** |

19 Enter the amount, if any, from line 18 of the **Unrecaptured Section 1250 Gain Worksheet** in
the instructions . . . . ▶ | **19** | 25,605.

20 Are lines 18 and 19 **both** zero or blank?

☐ **Yes.** Complete Form 1040 through line 42, and then complete the **Qualified Dividends and Capital Gain Tax Worksheet** in the instructions for Form 1040. **Do not** complete lines 21 and 22 below.

Tax based on ordinary rate

☒ **No.** Complete Form 1040 through line 42, and then complete the **Schedule D Tax Worksheet** in the instructions. **Do not** complete lines 21 and 22 below.

21 If line 16 is a loss, enter here and on Form 1040, line 13, the **smaller** of:

• The loss on line 16 or
• ($3,000), or if married filing separately, ($1,500)   . . . . | **21** |

Note. When figuring which amount is smaller, treat both amounts as positive numbers.

22 Do you have qualified dividends on Form 1040, line 9b?

☐ **Yes.** Complete Form 1040 through line 42, and then complete the **Qualified Dividends and Capital Gain Tax Worksheet** in the Instructions for Form 1040.

☐ **No.** Complete the rest of Form 1040.

Schedule **D** (Form 1040)

ILLUSTRATION 7.1

SCHEDULE E
(Form 1040)

Supplemental Income and Loss
(From rental real estate, royalties, partnerships,
S corporations, estates, trusts, REMICs, etc)
► Attach to Form 1040 or Form 1041.
► See Instructions for Schedule E (Form 1040).

Name(s) shown on return
Paul Myers

Your social security number
123-45-6789

Part I **Income or Loss From Rental Real Estate and Royalties**   Note. If you are in the business of renting personal property, use **Schedule C** or **C-EZ** (see instructions). Report farm rental income or loss from **Form 4835** on page 2, line 40.

1	List the type and location of each **rental real estate property:**	2	For each rental real estate property listed on line 1, did you or your family use it during the tax year for personal purposes for more than the greater of: • 14 days, **or** • 10% of the total days rented at fair rental value? (See instructions.)		Yes	No
A	Residential Property 717 Rocket Street			A		X
B				B		
C				C		

Income:			Properties			Totals
		A	B	C		(Add columns A, B, and C.)
3 Rents received	3	25,000.			3	25,000.
4 Royalties received	4				4	

Expenses:

5 Advertising	5					
6 Auto and travel (see instructions)	6					
7 Cleaning and maintenance	7					
8 Commissions.	8					
9 Insurance	9					
10 Legal and other professional fees. . . .	10					
11 Management fees	11					
12 Mortgage interest paid to banks, etc (see instructions)	12	6,000.			12	6,000.
13 Other interest.	13					
14 Repairs.	14					
15 Supplies	15					
16 Taxes	16					
17 Utilities	17	1,500.				
18 Other (list) ►	18					
19 Add lines 5 through 18	19	7,500.			19	7,500.
20 Depreciation expense or depletion (see instructions)	20	12,522.			20	12,522.
21 Total expenses. Add lines 19 and 20 . .	21	20,022.				
22 Income or (loss) from rental real estate or royalty properties. Subtract line 21 from line 3 (rents) or line 4 (royalties). If the result is a (loss), see instructions to find out if you must file **Form 6198**	22	4,978.				
23 Deductible rental real estate loss. **Caution.** Your rental real estate loss on line 22 may be limited. See instructions to find out if you must file **Form 8582**. Real estate professionals must complete line 43 on page 2	23					
24 **Income.** Add positive amounts shown on line 22. Do not include any losses					24	4,978.
25 **Losses.** Add royalty losses from line 22 and rental real estate losses from line 23. Enter total losses here					25	
26 **Total rental real estate and royalty income or (loss).** Combine lines 24 and 25. Enter the result here. If Parts II, III, IV, and line 40 on page 2 do not apply to you, also enter this amount on Form 1040, line 17. Otherwise, include this amount in the total on line 41 on page 2					26	4,978.

Schedule **E** (Form 1040)

ILLUSTRATION 7.1

Form **4797**		**Sales of Business Property** (Also Involuntary Conversions and Recapture Amounts Under Sections 179 and 280F(b)(2)) ► Attach to your tax return. ► See separate instructions.	

Name(s) shown on return	Identifying number
Paul Myers	123-45-6789

1 Enter the gross proceeds from sales or exchanges reported to you for 2004 on Form(s) 1099-B or 1099-S
(or substitute statement) that you are including on line 2, 10, or 20 (see instructions) . . . . | **1** |

Part I **Sales or Exchanges of Property Used in a Trade or Business and Involuntary Conversions From Other Than Casualty or Theft — Most Property Held More Than 1 Year** (see instructions)

2 (a) Description of property	(b) Date acquired (month, day, year)	(c) Date sold (month, day, year)	(d) Gross sales price	(e) Depreciation allowed or allowable since acquisition	(f) Cost or other basis, plus improvements and expense of sale	(g) Gain or (loss) Subtract (f) from the sum of (d) and (e)
Residential Rental Property Land	2/14/	10/20/	45,000.		15,000.	30,000.

Enter Land Here

3 Gain, if any, from Form 4684, line 39	**3**	
4 Section 1231 gain from installment sales from Form 6252, line 26 or 37	**4**	
5 Section 1231 gain or (loss) from like-kind exchanges from Form 8824	**5**	
6 Gain, if any, from line 32, from other than casualty or theft	**6**	85,605.
7 Combine lines 2 through 6. Enter the gain or (loss) here and on the appropriate line as follows	**7**	115,605.

Partnerships (except electing large partnerships) and S corporations. Report the gain or (loss) following the instructions for Form 1065, Schedule K, line 10, or Form 1120S, Schedule K, line 9. Skip lines 8, 9, 11, and 12 below.

All others. If line 7 is zero or a loss, enter the amount from line 7 on line 11 below and skip lines 8 and 9. If line 7 is a gain and you did not have any prior year section 1231 losses, or they were recaptured in an earlier year, enter the gain from line 7 as a long-term capital gain on Schedule D and skip lines 8, 9, 11, and 12 below.

8 Nonrecaptured net section 1231 losses from prior years (see instructions)	**8**	
9 Subtract line 8 from line 7. If zero or less, enter -0-. If line 9 is zero, enter the gain from line 7 on line 12 below. If line 9 is more than zero, enter the amount from line 8 on line 12 below and enter the gain from line 9 as a long-term capital gain on Schedule D (see instructions)	**9**	

Part II **Ordinary Gains and Losses**

10 Ordinary gains and losses not included on lines 11 through 16 (include property held 1 year or less):

11 Loss, if any, from line 7	**11**	
12 Gain, if any, from line 7 or amount from line 8, if applicable	**12**	
13 Gain, if any, from line 31	**13**	0.
14 Net gain or (loss) from Form 4684, lines 31 and 38a	**14**	
15 Ordinary gain from installment sales from Form 6252, line 25 or 36	**15**	
16 Ordinary gain or (loss) from like-kind exchanges from Form 8824	**16**	
17 Combine lines 10 through 16	**17**	0.

18 For all except individual returns, enter the amount from line 17 on the appropriate line of your return and skip lines a and b below. For individual returns, complete lines a and b below:

a If the loss on line 11 includes a loss from Form 4684, line 35, column (b)(ii), enter that part of the loss here. Enter the part of the loss from income-producing property on Schedule A (Form 1040), line 27, and the part of the loss from property used as an employee on Schedule A (Form 1040), line 22. Identify as from 'Form 4797, line 18a.' See instructions	**18a**	
b Redetermine the gain or (loss) on line 17 excluding the loss, if any, on line 18a. Enter here and on Form 1040, line 14	**18b**	0.

Form **4797**

ILLUSTRATION 7.1

Form **4797** Paul Myers				123-45-6789		Page **2**

Part III   Gain From Disposition of Property Under Sections 1245, 1250, 1252, 1254, and 1255

19 (a) Description of section 1245, 1250, 1252, 1254, or 1255 property:	**(b)** Date acquired (mo, day, yr)	**(c)** Date sold (mo, day, yr)
A Residential Rental Property	02/14/	10/20/
B Renovation	07/12/	10/20/
C		
D		

These columns relate to the properties on lines 19A through 19D .... ▶		Property A	Property B	Property C	Property D
20	Gross sales price (**Note:** See line 1 before completing.)	20	475,000.	50,000.	Enter Improvements Here	
21	Cost or other basis plus expense of sale	21	415,000.	50,000.		
22	Depreciation (or depletion) allowed or allowable .	22	23,333.	2,272.		
23	Adjusted basis. Subtract line 22 from line 21 ..	23	391,667.	47,728.		
24	Total gain. Subtract line 23 from line 20	24	83,333.	2,272.		
25	**If section 1245 property:**					
	a Depreciation allowed or allowable from line 22 .	25 a	Enter Building Here			
	b Enter the **smaller** of line 24 or 25a ...	25 b				
26	**If section 1250 property:** If straight line depreciation was used, enter -0- on line 26g, except for a corporation subject to section 291.					
	a Additional depreciation after 1975 (see instrs) . .	26 a	0.	0.		
	b Applicable percentage multiplied by the **smaller** of line 24 or line 26a (see instructions)	26 b				
	c Subtract line 26a from line 24. If residential rental property **or** line 24 is not more than line 26a, skip lines 26d and 26e	26 c	83,333.	2,272.		
	d Additional depreciation after 1969 & before 1976	26 d				
	e Enter the **smaller** of line 26c or 26d ..	26 e				
	f Section 291 amount (corporations only)	26 f				
	g Add lines 26b, 26e, and 26f.......	26 g	0.	0.		
27	**If section 1252 property:** Skip this section if you did not dispose of farmland or if this form is being completed for a partnership (other than an electing large partnership).					
	a Soil, water, and land clearing expenses	27 a				
	b Line 27a multiplied by applicable percentage (see instructions)	27 b				
	c Enter the **smaller** of line 24 or 27b ...	27 c				
28	**If section 1254 property:**					
	a Intangible drilling and development costs, expenditures for development of mines and other natural deposits, and mining exploration costs (see instructions)	28 a				
	b Enter the **smaller** of line 24 or 28a ...	28 b				
29	**If section 1255 property:**					
	a Applicable percentage of payments excluded from income under section 126 (see instructions)......	29 a				
	b Enter the **smaller** of line 24 or 29a (see instrs) .	29 b				

Summary of Part III Gains.   Complete property columns A through D through line 29b before going to line 30.

30	Total gains for all properties. Add property columns A through D, line 24	30	85,605.
31	Add property columns A through D, lines 25b, 26g, 27c, 28b, and 29b. Enter here and on line 13	31	0.
32	Subtract line 31 from line 30. Enter the portion from casualty or theft on Form 4684, line 33. Enter the portion from other than casualty or theft on Form 4797, line 6	32	85,605.

Part IV   Recapture Amounts Under Sections 179 and 280F(b)(2) When Business Use Drops to 50% or Less
(see instructions)

		(a) Section 179	**(b)** Section 280F(b)(2)
33	Section 179 expense deduction or depreciation allowable in prior years	33		
34	Recomputed depreciation. See instructions........................	34		
35	Recapture amount. Subtract line 34 from line 33. See the instructions for where to report	35		

Form **4797**

Chapter 8
MULTIPLE-UNIT HOMES

One of the best investments for first-time homebuyers is the purchase of a multi-family home. It enables the homebuyer to personally live in one of the units, benefit from the mortgage interest and property tax deductions, and exclude part of the gain on the sale of the home used for personal purposes. The other units can be used for rental purposes, allowing the homebuyer to produce rental income to defray some of the home expenses and benefit from all the rental deductions not permitted for personal homeowners. The only issue with owning a multi-unit home is that you will be required to follow two sets of tax rules. One set of IRS rules has to be followed for the personal home and the other set of rules has to be followed for residential rental part. All of these rules have been covered in the first seven chapters of this book. The only additional information that you need to know is how to identify, separate, and report the expenses of the personal part from the rental part.

The IRS rules are very simple when it comes to owning a property where you live in one of the units and rent out the other units. Think of this property as if you owned two separate pieces of property, one piece being the personal residence and the other piece being the rental property. With that understanding, simply apply all the rules regarding purchasing, owning, and selling a personal residence discussed in Part I of this book to the personal piece, and apply all the rules regarding purchasing, owning, and selling rental property discussed in Part II of this book to the rental piece.

Treatment of Tax Deductions

By now you should be aware that the tax rules for a personal residence are very different from the tax rules of rental property. Therefore, it is important that you identify and divide the expenses that are shared between the personal and rental parts. For instance, when you first buy a multi-unit home you will have to divide the purchase price of the home between both parts, because you will depreciate the cost of rental property on Schedule E but you cannot deduct the purchase price of a personal home.

The same holds true for mortgage interest and property taxes. Since there will be only one monthly interest statement and one property tax bill, you will have to divide the shared cost between the personal part and the rental part. Report the interest and property taxes of the personal part on Schedule A and the rental part on Schedule E. Also, if you heat the home, you have to divide the expense between the two pieces because heating costs of your rental property are deductible on Schedule E but are not deductible on a personal residence.

Shared repairs and common utilities also have to be divided so you can take the deduction for the rental piece on Schedule E. Please note that repairs done solely on the rental piece will be deducted in its entirety since it only relates to the rental part.

As you can see, the tax rules on multi-unit homes are the same for personal and rental properties. The only difference is that since it is only one structure you have to divide up all the shared costs between the personal and rental parts of the property.

How to Divide the Costs

The IRS allows you to use any reasonable method to divide shared costs. The key word here is *reasonable*. The most common ways are to divide shared costs based on the amount of rooms or square footage of the property. Although these methods may be the most common, they may not be the simplest ways. If the units are fairly equal in size, you may prefer to divide the costs based on the total number of units.

Example:

Omar purchased a four-family home and the units are fairly equal in size. He took out a mortgage to pay for the home and decided to live in one unit and rent out the other three. If Omar heated the entire home and replaced the lock on the door of one of the rental units, he would be able to deduct 25% of the mortgage interest for his personal piece on Schedule A and 75% of the mortgage interest for the rental piece on Schedule E. Since the door lock solely relates to the rental unit, he can deduct the entire amount on Schedule E. He also is allowed to deduct 75% of the heating expenses on Schedule E. He cannot deduct his personal heating part.

Selling

The same rules regarding the sale of personal and rental properties apply to a multi-unit property. Again, think of the multi-unit property as two separate pieces of property. The part used for personal purposes will follow the capital gain exclusion rules and reporting rules discussed in Chapter 3 of this book. The part used for rental purposes will be subject to ordinary and capital gain tax, and reporting rules discussed in Chapter 7. The only difference is that you will have to assign the selling price and purchase price of each part by dividing the amounts based on the same reasonable method used to divide the shared costs. For example, if you have a two-family home, with one unit used for personal purposes and the other for rental purposes, then simply assign half the selling and purchase price to each piece.

How to Treat a Room Rental

The IRS treats the sale of a personal home used in part for rental different from the sale of a multi-unit home. Very simply, the IRS allows you to apply the gain exclusion rules for a personal residence on the entire home as long as the part used for rental does not have a separate entrance. In addition, IRS Form 4797 does not have to be used to report the sale.

As a final comment, if you meet the tests discussed in Chapter 3, exclude up to $250,000 ($500,000 for married couples filing jointly), but do not exclude any depreciation taken in connection with the room rental. As you can see, depreciation is something that you will never escape. If you determine there is a gain after the exclusion or if you must report the tax on the depreciation taken, do so on Schedule D. After completing the worksheets in IRS Publication 523, report the gain, exclusion, and taxable gain on Schedule D.

Example:

Jim sold his personal home in 2007 at a $75,000 gain. He had rented one of the bedrooms to a friend since 2002, and deducted a total of $1,000 for depreciation that was attributable to the room rental. Jim also meets the ownership and use tests that allow him to exclude the gain of the home. According to IRS rules, Jim will be able to exclude up to $74,000 gain.

Chapter 9

Personal and Rental Use of Home

You may have a home that is used during the year for both personal and rental purposes, such as a vacation or second home. It is hard to label this hybrid of a home. Is it really a personal home used for rental activities, or is it a rental home used for personal activities?

The IRS labels such homes *dwelling units used as homes*, and depending on the number of days the home was used during the year for personal and rental purposes, different tax rules apply. The IRS considers a dwelling unit used as a home if you personally use it for more than fourteen days in a year or more than 10% of the total days rented.

Tax Rules on Vacation and Second Homes

To determine the tax treatment of a home used during the course of the year for personal and rental purposes, you first must determine whether the home is what the IRS considers a dwelling unit used as a home. To accomplish this, calculate the total number of days used for personal purposes and 10% of the total number of days it was rented. If it was personally used for more than fourteen days in a year or personally used for more than 10% of the total days rented, then it is considered a dwelling unit used as a home.

Look at the first part of the rule and determine whether a home was personally used for more than fourteen days. While you may think this may be simple, it is not. The IRS considers certain days used by other individuals to be personal days. If any of the following people use the unit, you must include these days as personal days. These individuals are:

- ***You or any co-owner of the unit.*** The exception to the co-owner using the unit is that he or she must be using it as a main home under an agreement known as a *shared equity financing agreement.* This is a fifty-year agreement that entitles the co-owner(s) to occupy the unit as long as the rent is paid to the other co-owner(s).
- ***Your family member or a family member of a co-owner of the unit.*** The IRS defines family members as siblings, half-brothers and -sisters, spouses, parents, grandparents, children, and grandchildren. However, if the family member pays a fair rental price, do not include these as personal days, because they are then considered rental days.
- ***Any individual that agrees to let you use another dwelling unit.*** For example, letting someone stay in your sky cabin for a stay in their summer bungalow.
- *Any person who pays less than a fair rental price.*

Next, calculate the total days rented. The IRS requires that you only include those days for which you received a *fair rental price.* A fair rental price would generally be the amount you would charge a non-family member and should be comparable to the rental amount charged by others for similar dwellings.

Example:

Ethan has an agreement with the local medical college to rent out his finished basement for the fall and spring semesters. He rents out the basement for a total of 240 days and receives fair market rent. Ethan allows his parents to live in the unit each year during their fourteen-day summer visit. According to the IRS rules, his parents' stay is considered personal use days.

The total personal use days is fourteen and 10% of the days rented is 24 days. Since Ethan did not use the unit for more than fourteen days or more than 10% of the rental days, the unit is not considered a dwelling unit used as a home. Rather, it is just a rental unit and all the activities should be reported as rental property.

Example:

Assume the same facts as the previous example, except that Ethan's parents used the unit for a total of twenty-one days. Since the unit was used for more than fourteen days, it automatically is considered a dwelling used as a home. Special tax rules apply on deducting rental expenses and reporting rental losses.

Example:

Mona rents a property to her daughter for the entire year. Mona's daughter uses the property as her main home and pays Mona a fair market price for the unit.

Although the unit is rented to a family member, Mona's daughter pays a fair market rental price for the rental. These days should not be considered personal use days, and instead the rental activities should be reported as any other rental property.

Example:

Pedro rented his Las Vegas condominium for 120 days during the year. He used the condominium twenty other days during the same year.

Pedro determined that the condominium was used personally for twenty days and that 10% of the total days it was rented to others was twelve days (10% of 120). Since Pedro personally used the condominium for more than 10% of the total rental days, the property is considered a dwelling unit used as a home. Special tax rules apply on deducting rental expenses and reporting rental losses.

Special Rules on Deductions

If the second home or vacation home that you personally used during the year is a dwelling unit used as a home, special tax rules apply. The amount of expenses on the property has to be divided between the personal use and the rental use. The IRS wants you to divide these expenses based on the total number of days the home was used for personal and rental purposes.

Example:

Jill rented her summer home for a fair market price for a total of seventy-five days. Jill also vacationed in the home for twenty-five other days during the same year. To determine the amount of expenses that should be divided to the rental and personal part, divide the rental days and personal days by the total days used for each purpose. In Jill's case, she will deduct 75% (75 days divided by 100 days) of the expenses for rental activities and 25% (25 days divided by 100 days) for personal expenses.

How to Report Expenses on a Dwelling Unit Used as a Home

Once you have determined—based on the fourteen-day, 10% rule—that you used a dwelling unit as a home and have divided the expenses, you need to know where to deduct these expenses. The percent of personal expenses should be deducted on Schedule A, and as you should know by now, these expenses are basically limited to mortgage interest and property taxes. You could never take a personal deduction for such items as utilities, repairs, or insurance.

However, the expenses that you determine to be rental activities should be reported along with the rental income on Schedule E. Here, you would deduct such items as utilities, repairs, and insurance.

Exception to the Rule

If you use the home for personal purposes and only rented it for less than fifteen days during the year, the IRS allows you to take the rent and put it in your pocket without having to report a single dime. However, you are not allowed to deduct any rental expenses.

Example:

Caleb owns a cabin in an exclusive Vermont lodge, which is mainly used as a vacation home. Caleb decided to rent the home for fourteen days to a friend for $3,000. If this is the only time during the year that the vacation home was rented, Caleb would not report any of the rental activities. He would take the money and run because it is tax-free. On the other hand, if Caleb had to pay someone $100 to clean up the cabin to get it ready for the renter, he would not be allowed to take that deduction. Still, Caleb does not mind, because he walks away with $2,900 of tax-free money.

Chapter 10
BUSINESS USE OF A HOME

One of the best jobs you can have is one that allows you to work from the coziness of your home. Imagine getting up in the morning and being able to show up to work by merely going into the next room. No more need to dress in a suit and tie and drive for an hour or get onto a crowded subway.

As professionals and experts become more and more in demand, many of them give up their nine-to-five and turn to consulting. Through amazing advances in technology, most consultants decide to work at home.

However, consultants are not the only ones who exclusively work at home. With employees burning out from the mundane routine of their job and the frustrations of working for a boss, many seek an alternative by starting a business. A home business is a popular means of starting a business venture because the costs associated with paying high rents sometimes make it impossible for the average person to start a business.

Also, with the increasing demands of our jobs, many employees find themselves steadily working at home as well as at the office.

Whether you are a consultant, business entrepreneur, or employee, there are expenses associated with working from home. The IRS allows you to deduct home business expenses as long as you meet certain requirements.

As a taxpayer, you should be able to deduct any allowable expenses that are available to you, including home business expenses. However, the IRS does not make it easy to claim home business expenses because of complicated requirements, calculations, and reporting rules. You should also be aware that home business activities are at high risk of being examined by the IRS. This chapter provides guidance on the requirements that have to be met to qualify for home business deductions, how to perform the calculations to determine the amount to claim, and the forms needed to report a home business. If you qualify for home business deductions, take care to strictly adhere to tax rules because of the risk of an audit involved in claiming such deductions.

Meeting the Tax Rules for Home Businesses

The IRS will allow you to deduct the expenses from the part of the home that is used for business if you meet certain requirements. The requirements for deducting home business expenses are much more stringent than the requirements for deducting expenses of rental property. The rules require that to claim an expense for a *trade or business use* of a home you must use part of the home exclusively and regularly as your principal place of business. While this requirement may sound straightforward, it is not, as each part has a specific meaning and set of rules.

Trade or Business Use

To meet the *trade or business use* requirement, part of the home must be used to conduct a trade or business activity. For example, you use part of your home to create and develop fashion designs that will be promoted and sold to prospective buyers. Since your activities relate to a trade or business, you meet the requirement.

However, not all profit-motivated activities done at home are in connection with a trade or business. If the activities are not in connection with a trade or business, you do not meet the requirement and no home expenses can be deducted. For example, you have a substantial amount of money invested in your 401(k) plan, which you monitor each day. Based on your research, you constantly move the investments at night on your home computer. Since these activities are only done for your benefit and not in connection with a trade or business, the expenses incurred from research, Internet, and equipment used to monitor these activities cannot be deducted.

Exclusive Use

To meet the *exclusive use* requirement, a designated area of the home has to be used to run the trade or business. The area must be a room or other separately identifiable space but does not have to be permanently separated by walls. If the area is used for both business and personal activities, you fail the exclusive use requirement and cannot deduct any home business expenses.

Example:
Raul, an architect, uses his smallest bedroom as a study to draw plans and review blueprints for his clients. The room is set up with his kids' video games, which they play when Raul is not working. The room is not exclusively used for a trade or business, so any home-related business expenses are not deductible.

There are a couple exceptions to the exclusive use requirement. You do not have to meet the exclusive use requirement if:

- part of the home is used for storage of inventory of product samples, or
- part of the home is used as a day care facility.

Regular Use

To meet the *regular use* requirement, the part of the home used for business must be used on a regular basis. Casual or occasional business use is not considered regular use. There may be many different types of business use, so consider the nature of the activities to determine if you are using the space on a regular basis.

Principal Place of Business

To meet the *principal place of business* requirement, your home must be the principal place of business for a trade or business. The IRS will allow you to have more than one business location for any given business, but if you want to deduct home business expenses the home location must be the primary location.

There are certain considerations that must be made to determine whether the space used in your home is a principal place of business, including:

- the significance of the activities conducted at each business location, and
- the amount of time spent at each business location.

In addition, to meet the principal place of business requirement, the part of the home used for business must be exclusively and regularly used for administrative or management activities, and no other fixed location can be used to substantially perform these activities. Examples of some of these administrative or management activities include:

- billing patients, clients, or customers;
- preparing bid proposals;
- paying bills;
- bookkeeping and recordkeeping;
- setting up appointments; and,
- preparing payroll.

However, performing administrative or management activities at other locations will not automatically disqualify your home office from being your principal place of business. The IRS specifically allows for the following situations.

- You have others conduct your administrative or management activities at locations other than your home; e.g., a billing company bills your customers from another location.
- You conduct administrative or management activities at places that are not fixed locations of your business, such as a car or a hotel room.
- You occasionally conduct minimal administrative or management activities at fixed locations outside your home.
- You conduct substantial nonadministrative or non-management business activities at a fixed location outside your home; e.g., providing services to customers, clients, or patients at a fixed location of the business outside of the home.
- You have suitable space to conduct administrative or management activities outside your home, but choose to use your home office for those activities.

Example:

Lester is a licensed electrician who owns his business. His time is mostly spent at office buildings installing electrical fixtures and certifying the buildings' electrical work. He uses his basement as a home office exclusively and regularly for the administrative and management activities of the business. At the home office, Lester answer phone calls, orders electrical supplies, and bills the customers. He also prepares and submits bid proposals for potential jobs. He does not perform any administrative and management activities at any other fixed location except for his home office. He does use an outside payroll service to prepare his payroll.

Lester's home office meets the principal place of business requirement because it is used to conduct the administrative and management activities of his electrical business and he does not perform any of these duties at another fixed location. Although another company does the payroll service, this does not disqualify Lester from meeting the principal place of business requirement. According to the rules, Lester will be permitted to deduct home office expenses.

Example:

Gene owns the exclusive rights to sell a patented heart monitor in the Northeast. It is Gene's job to try to sell the machine to all the hospital and medical facilities in the Northeast area. He exclusively and regularly uses his den at home as his office. In his office, he sets up appointments with prospective buyers and schedules all of his out-of-town sales meetings. He also prepares the monthly and quarterly sales reports for the corporate office. Since he is often on the road due to the nature of his business, he makes phone calls from the hotel room and prepares sales contracts on the plane.

Gene's home meets the principal place of business requirement because it is used to conduct the administrative and management activities and he does not perform any of these duties at another fixed location. Although Gene performs minimum administrative and management activities in the hotel and on the plane it does not disqualify him from meeting the principal place of business requirement. According to the rules, Gene will be permitted to deduct home office expenses.

Example:

Ruthann is a self-employed clinical therapist who provides patient therapy at three clinics. She has desk space at one of the clinics where she could perform administrative and management activities. Because Ruthann only goes to the clinic that provides her with the desk space two days a week, she chooses to perform most of the administrative and management activities of the trade in one of the rooms in her home. The room is exclusively and regularly used for administrative and management activities that include:

- scheduling patients and clinic facilities for treatment;

- billing insurance companies and patients;

- updating patient files;

- researching medical conditions; and,

- preparing and submitting required state medical reports.

The room used in the home meets the principal place of business requirement because it is used to conduct administrative and management activities and these activities are not substantially performed at another fixed location. Although Ruthann chose to use the home instead of the desk provided at the clinic, this does not disqualify her from meeting the principal place of business requirement. Also, conducting substantial non-administrative or non-management activities outside of the home office, such as treating patients, did not disqualify Ruthann from meeting the principal business requirement. According to the rules, Ruthann will be permitted to deduct home office expenses.

There are a couple of exceptions to the principal place of business requirement. You do not meet the principal place of business requirement if:

- part of the home is exclusively and regularly used as a place where you meet or deal with patients, clients, or customers in the normal course of your trade or business; or,
- the trade or business area is a separate structure that is not attached to the home.

Exceptions to the Exclusive Use and Principal Place of Business Rules

Recall that in order to meet the exclusive use requirement, the area must be a room or other separately identifiable space and cannot be used for both business and personal activities. However, if you use part of the home for the storage of inventory or product samples, you do not have to meet the exclusive requirement. You must meet the following conditions to receive this exception.

- You must be in the trade or business of selling products at wholesale or retail.
- You must keep the trade or business inventory or product samples in the home.
- Your home is the only fixed place where you conduct your trade or business.
- The home storage place is used on a regular basis.
- The storage space must be separately identifiable and suitable for storage.

Example:
Rosario's business is to buy discounted merchandise and sell it on eBay. Many items she acquires are deeply discounted off-season goods. She makes her profit by holding on to these

items until the next season, when they are in demand. Her home is the only fixed location where she conducts this business. The whole garage and a quarter of the basement is used to store the inventory items. Rosario sometimes uses the garage and base-ment for personal reasons. Since she meets the conditions above, the expenses for these areas are deductible.

You do not have to meet the principal place of business requirement if, in the normal course of your business, you meet patients, clients, or customers at your home. This exception applies even if you conduct your business at other locations as long as you use the part of your home exclusively and regularly for business. However, you must physically meet with patients, clients, and customers at the home, and their use of the home must be a substantial factor in conducting your business. Many accountants, doctors, and lawyers that have offices in their home and work at other locations meet these requirements.

Example:
Denise, an orthopedic doctor, works two days in the hospital and has a practice that she runs out of her home. She uses the first floor of the home to exclusively and regularly see and treat patients. The exception applies and her home qualifies for business expenses deductions since patients are physically met and their use of the home is an important factor in conducting the business.

Another exception to the principal place of business requirement is when you conduct your business exclusively and regularly in a separate structure not attached to the home, such as a studio, garage, or barn.

Example:
Joey owns and runs the town's car and repair shop. He also uses a large free-standing garage at home exclusively and regularly to work on special projects for his customers. Joey is entitled to deduct the expenses of the home garage.

Treatment of Tax Deductions

The tax treatment used for deducting home business expenses is very similar to the rules on multi-unit rental homes. There are some expenses, such as a dedicated business phone, that are exclusively expenses of the business and can be deducted in their entirety. However, there are many expenses that are shared with the personal part of the home, such as the utility bill. You must be able to identify and divide the expenses that are shared between the personal and business part of the home. This is important because while qualifying home business expenses are deductible, most personal home expenses are not. You will have to know how to divide up the cost between the personal and business parts. For example, mortgage interest and property taxes are a shared expense. Since there will be only one monthly interest statement and one property tax bill, you will have to divide the shared cost between the personal part and the business part.

You should also be aware of the types of home business expenses you are allowed to deduct and the limitations on the amount you are able to deduct.

How to Divide the Costs

The IRS allows you to use any reasonable method to divide shared costs. The key word here is *reasonable*. The most common ways are to divide shared costs based on the amount of rooms or square footage of the property. Although these are the most common methods, they may not be the simplest ways. If the units are fairly equal in size, you may prefer to divide the costs based on the total number of units.

Either method will allow you to determine the business percentage of the home. Use this percentage to divide the shared expenses of the home. For example, if you use one out of five rooms equal in size to conduct business, the business percentage to apply to shared expenses is 20% (1 divided by 5).

Types of Deductions

There are two types of home expenses associated with home businesses. Expenses can be either direct or indirect to the operations of a business. *Direct expenses* are those costs that are generally not shared with the personal part of the home and can easily be identifiable to the operations of the business. The entire amount of direct expenses is deductible.

Example:
Jed runs his catering business from the basement of his home. He needs to install a special exhaust fan to control the smoke caused by the cooking. The exhaust fan costs him $150. The cost of the exhaust fan is clearly a direct expense to the operations of the business, and as such Jed is able to deduct the entire $150.

Indirect expenses are those costs that are generally shared with the personal part of the home. You must divide the cost of these expenses based on the percentage of business use discussed on the previous page. Indirect costs include real estate taxes, homeowners insurance, and utilities.

Example:
Tim uses 20% of his home for business during the entire year. If the annual utility bill was $1,000, then Tim will be able to claim $200 as a business expense.

Types of Expenses

There are several factors to consider when determining whether the type of business expense is direct or indirect and whether you may claim the entire expense or a business percentage. Following are a few examples of some home business expenses to help clarify which ones are direct or indirect and how much you are able to claim.

Mortgage Interest

Mortgage interest is generally a shared expense. If you use part of your home for a qualifying trade or business, you will be able to deduct the amount of mortgage interest based on the percentage of the home that is used for business. However, you should be aware that mortgage interest is generally deductible anyway. The only difference is that the amount is divided up between the personal part and the business part, and reported in two different areas of the tax return. So in reality there is no benefit to claiming a business expense for mortgage interest. Another thing that you should be aware of is that the same limits placed on deducting mortgage interest on an individual return apply to claiming mortgage interest as a business expense. If your mortgage loan is more than $1,000,000 or if your home equity loan is more than $100,000, then your deduction may be limited. See Chapter 2 for a discussion on these limitations.

Real Estate Taxes

Real estate taxes are generally a shared expense. If you use part of your home for a qualifying trade or business you will be able to deduct the amount of real estate taxes based on the percentage of the home used for business. However, similar to mortgage interest, real estate taxes are generally deductible anyway. The only difference is that the amount is divided up between the personal part and the business part, and reported in two different areas of the tax return. So in reality there is no benefit to claiming a business expense for real estate taxes.

Insurance

Homeowners insurance is generally a shared expense. If you use part of your home for a qualifying trade or business, you will be able to deduct the amount of insurance based on the percentage of time the home is used for business. However, the insurance deduction can be a little tricky. The IRS does not allow you to deduct as a business expense the part of the insurance premium that extends after the end of the year. This could be an issue for people who pay their insurance policies at the middle to end of the year. For example, you determine that the business percentage use of your home is 40%. Your insurance premium is due each year on July 1 and it continues through June 30 of the next year. If the premium is $1,000 you would first apply the business percentage to the total amount paid and find out the business expense is $400. Secondly, you would have to reduce this amount by half because only six months of the expense benefits the current year. So the amount that you are ultimately allowed to deduct is $200. To keep this simple, the ideal is to have your insurance policy cover the period between January 1 and December 31.

Repairs

The total amount of direct repairs that benefit only the business should be claimed as a business expense. This includes the painting and repairing of items only in the area used for business. However, general repairs are usually a shared expense. If you use part of your home for a qualifying trade or business, you may be able to deduct the amount of certain general repairs based on the percentage of the home used for business. For example, you use 15% of your home for business and had to repair your air and heating unit. You will be able to claim 15% of the repairs as a business expense. Remember that a repair is an expense paid to keep the rental property in working condition and adds no significant value to the property. Do not confuse repairs with improvements. Improvements have to be depreciated, as discussed later in this chapter.

Security System

Security systems that monitor the entire home, including the business part, are generally a shared expense. If you use part of your home for a qualifying trade or business you will be able to deduct the amount of the security monitoring expense based on the percentage the home is used for business. If you install a new system, you will be able to depreciate the costs associated with business use of the home.

Utilities and Services

Utilities and services include expenses such as electricity, oil, gas, trash removal, and cleaning services. These types of expenses are generally a shared expense. If you use part of your home for a qualifying trade or business you will be able to deduct the amount of utilities and services cost based on the percentage of the home used for business.

Telephone

The service charges and taxes for the first telephone line in your home are not deductible, even if the line is used partially for business purposes. However, the long distance charges made on the first line and the cost of having a second line used exclusively for business is a direct expense of the business. You may be able to deduct these expenses if you use part of your home for a qualifying trade of business.

Depreciation

Depreciation is simply a way the IRS looks at certain expenses and tells you how and when to deduct them. In the course of doing business you will purchase certain items that will have a useful life of more than one year. Since these items have a usefulness of more than one year, the IRS does not allow you to deduct the total expense in the year it is paid. Instead, you can only deduct a portion of the expense each year as prescribed by the IRS until the total cost is fully deducted. See Chapter 5 for a detailed discussion on depreciation.

There are three main expense deductions that have special treatment through the depreciation rules. These deductions are for the cost associated with:

- the value of the home that is used for business;
- permanent improvements; and,
- business furniture and equipment.

The Cost of the Home

One of the most substantial business expenses will be the cost of the part of the home that is used for business. The IRS will allow you to deduct the cost of the part of the home used for business equally over thirty-nine years. To determine the amount of the home that can be depreciated and claimed as a business expense you will first have to know:

- the month and year that the home business was started;
- the adjusted cost and fair market value of the home when the business was first started;
- the cost of any improvement before you started to use the home for business; and,
- the business percentage of the home that is used for business.

The month you began the business is fairly easy to figure out and by now you should have already calculated the business percentage as discussed in the previous section.

The *adjusted cost* is simply the original cost of the home plus any improvement before you began using the home for business. However, do not include the cost of land in the adjusted cost. The IRS rules have made it clear that the cost of land can never be deducted because land does not get used up, become obsolete, or wear out. You can find the cost of the home (excluding the land) in the sales contract or you can calculate it through the real estate assessment values.

The *fair market value* of the home at the time you began the business is the amount for which a buyer is willing to buy the property and the seller is willing to sell the property. You can use the real estate tax assessment values to quickly determine the fair market value of the home. Remember to exclude land amount.

Once you have all the information needed, you are ready to determine the amount of the home that can be depreciated. To calculate the depreciation deduction, multiply the business percentage from the date you began the business by the lesser of:
- the adjusted cost (excluding land), or
- the fair market value of your home.

The best way to depreciate the business cost of the home is to first determine the monthly depreciation amount. Simply take the cost of the building and divide it by 468 months (thirty-nine years). However, in the first year you begin the business, use the following table to figure out your depreciation deduction.

39-Year Depreciation Table

First Month Business Started	Multiplier
January	2.461%
February	2.247%
March	2.033%
April	1.819%
May	1.605%
June	1.391%
July	1.177%
August	0.963%
September	0.749%
October	0.535%
November	0.321%
December	0.107%

Example:

In September, Lou started to see his patients in one of the rooms in his home. He determined that the business percentage use of the home is 15%. Several years ago he bought the home exclusive of the land for $511,000. He determined that $19,000 worth of permanent improvements were made to the home prior to starting the business. According to the facts, Lou's adjusted cost of the home is $530,000.

He also determined that the fair market value exclusive of the land at the time he started the home business in September was $673,000. Selecting the lesser of the two, he multiplied the adjusted cost of $530,000 by the business percentage of 15%, which resulted in a total depreciable cost of $79,500.

To determine the amount of deduction that Lou is able to take in the first year, he must multiply the total depreciable cost of $79,500 by .00749, the multiplier for September from the table. Based on the calculation, Lou will be able to claim a depreciation deduction of $595.46.

The Cost of Permanent Improvements

Permanent improvements are very different from repairs. You must be able to distinguish between the two. Home business repairs are deducted in the year they are paid, while improvement expenses have to be depreciated over time.

The IRS defines a *repair* as an expense that keeps the home in good working condition. For example, if your kitchen faucet is leaking and you have to replace the handle to get it to properly work again, then the IRS considers the expense a repair. The IRS defines an *improvement* as an expense that adds value to the home, extends the useful life of what was improved, or adapts to new uses in the home. See the "Repairs vs. Improvements" section in Chapter 2 for examples of improvements.

Example:

Marina converts her garage to a fortune telling parlor. To get the place ready for business, she had to remodel the area, which included putting in new light fixtures, replacing the garage door with an entrance door, patching the walls, painting the room with dark colors, repairing the electrical outlets, and replacing the floor. Clearly the new light fixtures, new doors, and new floors are all improvements. Usually, patching walls, painting, and fixing the outlets are all repairs; however, since the remodeling work adapted the garage to a new use, the entire job is considered an improvement.

Improvements done before you began the business have to be added to the adjusted cost of the home. Improvements made after you begin using the home for business purposes are depreciated separately. If the improvement is shared with the personal part of the home, make sure to divide the cost. Depreciate all home business improvements equally over thirty-nine years. Use the 39-Year Depreciation Table on page 141 to calculate the first year deduction.

Business Furniture and Equipment

There are special tax rules for property bought for business use. The IRS does not allow you to immediately take the deduction on items that have a useful life of more than one year. Furniture and equipment are items that clearly have a useful life of more than one year. However, there is a special tax rule known as a Section 179 deduction. The tax code provides the taxpayer with the ability to deduct the entire cost of depreciable tangible items bought for use in a trade or business even if that business is run out of the taxpayer's home. In fact, the tax code gives you the following options:

- elect to take a Section 179 deduction for the entire cost of the item;
- depreciate the full cost of the item; or
- take a partial 179 deduction and depreciate the remaining balance.

The rule is flexible on how to deduct for business property. You can claim the entire deduction or choose how much to deduct immediately and depreciate the balance. If you choose to depreciate part or all of the expense, be aware that most business property used in a home office is depreciated over five or seven years.

- Computers and peripheral equipment, typewriters, calculators, adding machines, and copiers are usually depreciated over five years.
- Office furniture, desks, files, and safes are usually depreciated over seven years.

The depreciation method prescribed by the IRS for business property can be found in IRS Publication 946, or you can simply use a reputable tax program to figure out the depreciation amount.

Deduction Limit

If your home business breaks even or with a *profit* (gross income is equal to or greater than the operating expenses), you will be able to deduct all the home business expenses. It is when the business results in a loss (the gross income is less than operating expenses) that you have a problem. If the home business gross income is less than the expenses, limits are placed on certain home business expenses.

The limits are specifically placed on those expenses of the home that would not be deductible if the home was not used for business purposes. These are usually shared expenses and include insurance, utilities, and depreciation on the adjusted cost of the home.

Limits are not placed on home business expenses like home mortgage interest and real estate taxes because these items are deductible regardless if you have a home business or not. Also, direct business expenses such as a business phone, inventory, and depreciation of business equipment are not limited. You should know that generally business losses are not limited on a business that is not home-based. The restrictions placed by the IRS will restrict individuals that have costly home costs to claim these expenses on a losing business.

Expense Carryover

If you are not able to take all the home business expenses because of the limits imposed, you will be able to carry over any unallowed expenses. Therefore, you really never lose the benefit of those unallowed deductions. Use IRS Form 8829 to report any carryover deductions. Before you can report any carryover deductions, you have to calculate the limit in a manner prescribed by the IRS.

Determining the Limit

Automatically, if the business operates at a loss because the gross income was less than the business expenses, a calculation on the limit of home business expenses will have to be done. To determine the deduction limit, the IRS wants you to subtract those business expenses (insurance, utilities, and depreciation) that would normally not be deductible if you did not have a home business from the following:

- mortgage interest and real estate taxes, and
- direct expenses that relate to the business.

Example:

Joseph met all the requirements for deducting expenses on the part of his home that is used for business. He determined that the business use percentage is 10% for home-related business expenses shared with the personal part of the home. Joseph used the following IRS model to determine the expense limit.

Gross Income from the business $10,000

Minus:
Deductible mortgage interest
and real estate taxes (10%) 2,500
Direct business expenses not related to the use
of the home (100%), such as business phone,
inventory, and depreciation of business equipment . .6,500

Limit on home related business deduction . . . . . .**$ 1,000**

Minus shared home expenses:
Maintenance, insurance, utilities (10%) 900
Depreciation on cost of home and improvements (10%),
depreciation expense at 10% was $2,000 but could only
claim up to the limit 100
Other expenses up the deduction limit . . . .**$ 1,000**

Depreciation carryover ($2,000 $100) . . . .**$ 1,900**

Joseph is able to deduct $2,500 of the mortgage interest and
real estate taxes on the part of the home used for business
purposes. He will also be able to deduct $6,500 for all the
direct business expenses not related to the use of the home.
He has a remaining $1,000 that he can apply to shared home
business expenses, of which he uses $900 for the mainte-
nance, insurance, and utility costs and $100 for only part of
the depreciation amount. The remaining unallowed depreciation expense of $1,900 may be carried forward to the next
year. Any unallowed carryover expenses are subject to the
same limits in the next year.

Where to Deduct

Home businesses can operate under many forms, such as a sole
proprietorship, corporation, or partnership. However, the most
common and inexpensive way to operate a small home business is
under a sole proprietorship. A sole proprietorship is a business
organization in which the individual and company are treated as a
single entity for tax and liability purposes. The following discussion will focus on where to report home business activities for a
sole proprietorship.

If you are self-employed and operate as a sole proprietor, your home business activities will be reported on IRS Form 1040 by using supplemental Schedule C, "Profit or Loss From Business" and Form 8829, "Expenses for Business Use of Your Home." Use Part I of Form 8829 to report the percentage of the home used for business. Complete Part II to figure out and report all home-related business expenses. This part is also used to determine the deduction limit. Complete Part III to calculate the depreciation and Part IV to report any carryover of unallowed expenses.

Once Form 8829 is completed, transfer the amount you are allowed to claim on line 34 to Schedule C. Also use Schedule C to report the gross income and any other business expense that is not associated with the home. The result of Schedule C is transferred to IRS Form 1040.

Using the facts for Joseph's home business on page 145, see Illustration 10.1 for an example on how to report home business expenses.

Day Care Facility

There are special tax rules that apply to operating a day care out of your home when you use areas of the home that are also used for non-business purposes. This section explains the tax rules and gives guidance on how to calculate and report home business deductions under these circumstances.

If you operate a day care facility out of your home, you do not need to meet the exclusive use rule that requires you to have a designated area of the home used exclusively for business. A home day care business may operate out of areas in your home that are also used for personal purposes, as long as the space is used regularly for the business. To qualify for the exclusive use exception, the following IRS requirements must be met.

- You must be engaged in the trade or business of providing day care to children, individuals 65 years of age or older, or individuals who are physically or mentally unable to care for themselves.
- You must have applied for, been issued, or be exempt from having a state license, certification, registration, or approval as a family or group day care home. This requirement is not met if your application is rejected or your license, certification, or approval has been revoked.

Determining the Deduction

As with any other home business, you will have several expenses that are shared with the personal part of the home. You will have to divide these expenses based on the amount of space used in the home for business purposes to determine a business use percentage. This percentage is used to allocate the shared cost to the business part. If you use part of the home exclusively for operating the day care, you would simply multiply the business use percentage to the shared expenses and deduct the results like any other home business.

However, if you elect the exclusive use exemption and operate the business in areas of the home that are also used for non-business purposes, a further reduction of indirect home expenses will have to be calculated based on the time you actually used the space for business. For a room that is used both for operating the day care and non-business purposes, to qualify for any type of deduction it must be used regularly for business and occasionally for personal purposes.

To determine the deduction that is allowed when the rooms are not exclusively used for the day care, you will first need to know the percentage of the home that is used for business. There are two acceptable methods to calculate the business use percentage. You can divide the square footage of the business area by the total area of the home, or if the rooms are of equal size, divide the rooms used for business by the total amount of rooms in the home. You will also need to calculate the percentage of time that the home was actually used for business. To accomplish this, compare the total number of hours the home was used for business during the year to the total number of hours in a year. Please note that the IRS does not require you to keep detailed records on the specific time the home was used for business.

Once you calculate the business percentage and the time percentage, deduct any direct expenses of the home by the time percentage. Any shared expenses have to be reduced by both the business and time percentage.

Example:

Lillian uses her fully equipped first floor to operate a day care. Her home has a total of four levels. The first floor is used occasionally for personal purposes. She uses the square footage of the home to calculate the business percentage.

Business Percentage

Square footage of the first floor		1,000
Square footage of the home		4,000
	=	25%

The day care business is open five days a week, twelve hours a day for the entire year. The first floor is available for use after business hours and weekends. The percentage of time the first floor was actually used for business is as follows.

Time Percentage

Hours used for day care (12 x 5 x 52)	3,120
Total hours in a year (24 x 365 days)	8,760
=	35.6%

Now that Lillian has both percentages, she has one last calculation. That is the combined percentage that will be used to determine the deduction for indirect expenses.

Combined Percentage

Business Percentage (25%) x Time Percentage (35.61%) = 8.9%

Now Lillian has painfully calculated all the percentages needed to figure the amount she can deduct. She will be able to deduct 35.6% of the direct home expenses and 8.9% of the indirect business expenses shared with the personal part of the home.

The maximum direct home expense that can be claimed is 35.6% because the first floor was not exclusively used for the day care. Direct home expenses include repairs to the first floor and depreciation of improvements after the business was started.

The maximum amount of indirect expenses that can be claimed is 8.9% because these expenses are shared with the entire home. Indirect expenses include mortgage interest, property taxes, homeowners insurance, general repairs and maintenance, and depreciation expenses for the cost of the home.

The amount of business expenses not related to the use of the home can be claimed at 100%. These expenses include the business phone, toys and books for the children, and business equipment.

Where to Deduct Home Day Care Expenses

If you are a self-employed day care provider, report the business activities under IRS Form 1040 by using supplemental Schedule C, "Profit or Loss From Business," and Form 8829, "Expenses for Business Use of Your Home." Use Part I of Form 8829 to calculate the business use and time percentage. Complete Part II and Part III to figure out and report all home-related business expenses.

Once Form 8829 is completed, transfer the amount you are allowed to claim on line 34 to Schedule C. Also use Schedule C to report the gross income and any other business expenses that are not associated with the home. Transfer the results of Schedule C to IRS Form 1040.

Employees

If you work for someone and perform job duties at home, you may be able to deduct home-related business expenses. You would have to meet certain requirements, and of course these expenses can not be reimbursed by your employer. Employee-related home business expenses are not reported on the same IRS forms as those of self-employed individuals.

Qualifying Requirements

To claim this deduction, you will have to the meet the exclusive use, regular use, and principal place of business requirements discussed in the beginning of this chapter. For employees, the IRS requires two additional requirements.

- Your business use must be for the convenience of your employer.
- You must not rent any part of your home to your employer and use the rented portion to perform services as an employee to the employer.

If you conduct job-related tasks in a home office just because it is appropriate and helpful, the home business expenses are not deductible.

Example:
Nancy is employed as a speech therapist with the Westchester County School District. She diagnoses and treats the students in an office provided by her employer. She is also required to document the progress of her cases. The school district provides her with an office computer and supplies to do the necessary documentation. Although Nancy is able to document her cases in the office provided by the school district, she prefers to do all the documentation in her home office. Her home office was exclusively used for this purpose. Her employer does not require her to work at home.

Nancy has met the exclusive use, regular use, and principal place of business requirement. However, she did not meet the convenience-to-the-employer requirement. Since her employer provides her with an office to perform her documentation duties and does not require her to work at home, she does not meet the convenience-to-the-employer requirement and will not be able to claim any home business deductions.

Reporting Home Business Expenses as an Employee

Unlike a self-employed individual, where all the activities are reported on IRS Form Schedule C and Form 8829, employees qualifying home business deductions are reported on IRS Form Schedule A, "Itemized Deductions." The problem with using Schedule A to deduct home business expenses is that taxpayers are only allowed to take the greater of the following types of deductions.

- Itemized deductions are certain personal expenses including charitable contributions, points, mortgage interest, state withholding taxes, property taxes, and unreimbursed employer business expenses.
- The standard deduction is a fixed deduction set by the IRS and based on your filing status of single, head of household, married filing jointly, married filing separately, or qualifying widower.

Generally, if you own a home your itemized deductions will be greater than your standard deduction. However, if your standard deduction is greater, it would not make sense to itemize, and although those home business expenses are deductible, they did nothing to benefit you on the tax return.

Where to Deduct Home Business Expenses as an Employee

Deductible Mortgage Interest

Since personal mortgage interest is deductible on Schedule A and employee home business expenses are also deductible on Schedule A, simply enter the total amount of deductible mortgage interest on line 10 or 11 of Schedule A. Just remember that the limits placed on deducting mortgage interest apply regardless if the home is used for personal or business use. If your mortgage loan is more than $1,000,000 or home equity loan is more than $100,000, then your deduction may be limited. See Chapter 2 for a discussion on these limitations.

Real Estate Taxes

As with mortgage interest, both personal and business real estate expenses are deductible on Schedule A. Report all of the real estate taxes paid on line 6 of Schedule A.

Other Home Business Expenses

Line 20 of Schedule A is where you will report all shared and direct home business expenses. Other home business expenses include homeowners insurance, utilities, repairs, and the cost of improvements. The business use percentage and deduction limits that apply to regular home businesses also apply here. If you have additional unreimbursed employee expenses that do not involve the home, such as travel and parking, you would need to complete IRS Form 2106, "Unreimbursed Business Expenses," to report everything. If you use Form 2106, enter the home-related business expenses on line 4. It is best to use a reputable tax program to prepare these schedules. One last fact that you need to know about using line 20 of Schedule A to report your home business expenses is that the amount is reduced by 2% of your adjusted gross income.

Sale of Home

If you sell your residential property and it was used partly for business, the amount of tax paid on the gain depends on whether the home business is operated in part of the home or in a separate free-standing structure, such as a studio, garage, or barn. The IRS form used to report the sale also depends on these same factors. The tax amount charged on the sale of a home that was used partly for business is much less than the amount charged if a separate free-standing part of the property was used for business. Also, reporting the sale on the part of the home business is much simpler than if the business use was separate.

Sale of Home Partly Used for Business

If you use part of the home for business, such as a room or basement as a home office, you may be able to use the tax shelter rules provided in the 1997 Tax Relief Act. This law allows you to exclude up to $250,000 ($500,000 if you file a joint return as a married couple) on the gain from the sale of a personal residence. You would have to meet the ownership and use tests, which requires that within five years from the date of the sale you meet:

- the ownership test (you owned the home for at least two years), and
- the use test (you lived in the home for at least two years).

See Chapter 3 for a detailed discussion of the exclusion rules under the 1997 Tax Relief Act.

The only other issue that you would have to address is the depreciation deducted for the home cost and improvements, which were attributable to the business part of the home. Although the IRS allows you to exclude the gain if you meet the tests discussed above, it will not allow you to exclude the previously deducted depreciation. Report the gain, exclusion, and taxable amount due to depreciation only on IRS Form Schedule D.

Example:

James sold his personal residence and determined that he had a $150,000 gain. He met both the ownership and use tests so he qualified for the gain exclusion. However, he used his basement for the past few years to operate a home-based tax practice. He looked back at his records and determined that the depreciation previously deducted for the home cost and improvements attributable to the business was $10,000. James would have to report the gain and exclusion of only $140,000 ($150,000 − $10,000), and capital gain of $10,000. As you can see, the amount taxed on the sale of the personal residence is only $10,000.

Sale of Home of Separate Part of Home Used for Business

If you sell property for which a separate part of the property was used for business, then the part of the property used for business does not qualify for the exclusion rules and you would have to pay taxes on some of the gain. To determine the tax treatment on a property for which a separate part of the home was used to operate a business, it is best to treat the property as if it were two separate properties. The part used for personal purposes will follow the capital gain exclusion rules and reporting rules discussed in Chapter 3 of this book. The part used for business will be subject to ordinary and capital gain tax, and reporting rules as if it was a rental property, discussed in Chapter 6 of this book. The only difference is that you will have to assign the selling price and purchase price of each part by dividing the amounts based on the business use percentage.

Example:

Lisa, a self-employed author, bought a property several years ago that included a main home and a small one-room guest-house that was separate from the home. She lived in the home and used the guesthouse as a home office to do her writing, editing, and administrative work. She sold the home for a $75,000 gain and determined that $60,000 of the gain was personal and $15,000 of the gain was business.

She would take the exclusion for the personal part and would have to report the sale of the business part on IRS Form 4797. If she previously depreciated $6,000 as a home business expense, ordinary income tax rates are charged on that amount and capital gain taxes will be charged on the remaining balance of $9,000.

As you can see, selling residential property for which a separate part of the home was used for business causes complex calculations to determine the gain and involves difficult reporting requirements. There is a solution—if you meet the ownership and use tests before you sell the home, then you would only have to pay taxes on what was depreciated. So if you plan to sell the home and do not meet both ownership and use tests, consider using the home entirely for personal purposes until you satisfy the requirements. Be aware that if you sell the home in the same year that you used it for business, you cannot use the exclusion rules on the business part, even if you meet the ownership and use tests.

ILLUSTRATION 10.1

Form **1040**	Department of the Treasury — Internal Revenue Service **U.S. Individual Income Tax Return**	

For the year Jan 1 - Dec 31,   , or other tax year beginning

Label
(See instructions.)

Use the IRS label.
Otherwise, please print or type.

Your first name: JOSEPH   MI   Last name: HOMEBIZ

If a joint return, spouse's first name   MI   Last name

Home address (number and street). If you have a P.O. box, see instructions.   Apartment no.
2200 RODEO DRIVE

City, town or post office. If you have a foreign address, see instructions.   State   ZIP code
SAINT LOUIS   MO   99999

Your social security number: 070-88-0011

Spouse's social security number

▲ **Important!** ▲
You **must** enter your social security number(s) above.

Presidential Election Campaign
(See instructions.)
▶ Note: Checking 'Yes' will not change your tax or reduce your refund.
Do you, or your spouse if filing a joint return, want $3 to go to this fund? .... ▶
You: Yes [ ] No [ ]   Spouse: Yes [ ] No [ ]

Filing Status

Check only one box.

1 [X] Single
2 [ ] Married filing jointly (even if only one had income)
3 [ ] Married filing separately. Enter spouse's SSN above & full name here. ▶
4 [ ] Head of household (with qualifying person). (See instructions.) If the qualifying person is a child but not your dependent, enter this child's name here ▶
5 [ ] Qualifying widow(er) with dependent child (see instructions)

Exemptions

6a [X] Yourself. If someone can claim you as a dependent, **do not** check box 6a. ....
b [ ] Spouse ....

c Dependents:

(1) First name Last name	(2) Dependent's social security number	(3) Dependent's relationship to you	(4) ✔ if qualifying child for child tax credit (see instrs)
			[ ]
			[ ]
			[ ]
			[ ]

If more than four dependents, see instructions.

Boxes checked on 6a and 6b . 1
No. of children on 6c who:
● lived with you . . .
● did not live with you due to divorce or separation (see instrs) . .
Dependents on 6c not entered above .
Add numbers on lines above . . ▶   1

d Total number of exemptions claimed   1

Income

Attach Form(s) W-2 here. Also attach Forms W-2G and 1099-R if tax was withheld.

If you did not get a W-2, see instructions.

Enclose, but do not attach, any payment. Also, please use Form 1040-V.

7 Wages, salaries, tips, etc. Attach Form(s) W-2   7
8 a Taxable interest. Attach Schedule B if required 8a
  b Tax-exempt interest. **Do not** include on line 8a 8b
9 a Ordinary dividends. Attach Schedule B if required 9a
  b Qualifd divs (see instrs) 9b
10 Taxable refunds, credits, or offsets of state and local income taxes (see instructions)   10
11 Alimony received.   11
12 Business income or (loss). Attach Schedule C or C-EZ.   12   0.
13 Capital gain or (loss). Att Sch D if reqd. If not reqd, ck here .... ▶ [ ]   13
14 Other gains or (losses). Attach Form 4797   14
15 a IRA distributions ....   15a   b Taxable amount (see instrs) . .   15b
16 a Pensions and annuities . . .   16a   b Taxable amount (see instrs) . .   16b
17 Rental real estate, royalties, partnerships, S corporations, trusts, etc. Attach Schedule E . . .   17
18 Farm income or (loss). Attach Schedule F   18
19 Unemployment compensation   19
20 a Social security benefits ......   20a   b Taxable amount (see instrs) . .   20b
21 Other income   21
22 Add the amounts in the far right column for lines 7 through 21. This is your **total income** . . ▶   22   0.

Transfer from Schedule C Line 31

Adjusted Gross Income

23 Educator expenses (see instructions)   23
24 Certain business expenses of reservists, performing artists, and fee-basis government officials. Attach Form 2106 or 2106-EZ   24
25 IRA deduction (see instructions)   25
26 Student loan interest deduction (see instructions)   26
27 Tuition and fees deduction (see instructions).   27
28 Health savings account deduction. Attach Form 8889   28
29 Moving expenses. Attach Form 3903.   29
30 One-half of self-employment tax. Attach Schedule SE   30
31 Self-employed health insurance deduction (see instrs)   31
32 Self-employed SEP, SIMPLE, and qualified plans   32
33 Penalty on early withdrawal of savings   33
34 a Alimony paid b Recipient's SSN. . . ▶   34a
35 Add lines 23 through 34a   35
36 Subtract line 35 from line 22. This is your **adjusted gross income** .... ▶   36   0.

BAA For Disclosure, Privacy Act, and Paperwork Reduction Act Notice, see instructions.   Form **1040**

ILLUSTRATION 10.1

SCHEDULE A (Form 1040)		**Itemized Deductions**				
Department of the Treasury Internal Revenue Service		▶ **Attach to Form 1040.** ▶ **See Instructions for Schedule A (Form 1040).**				

Name(s) shown on Form 1040 — JOSEPH HOMEBIZ

Your social security number — 070-88-0011

Medical and Dental Expenses		**Caution.** Do not include expenses reimbursed or paid by others.			
	1	Medical and dental expenses (see instructions)	1		
	2	Enter amount from Form 1040, line 37 . . .	2		
	3	Multiply line 2 by 7.5% (.075)	3		
	4	Subtract line 3 from line 1. If line 3 is more than line 1, enter -0-	4	
Taxes You Paid (See instructions.)	5	State and local (**check only one box**): a ☐ Income taxes, **or** b ☒ General sales taxes (see instructions)	5	224.
	6	Real estate taxes (see instructions)	6	4,500.
	7	Personal property taxes	7	
	8	Other taxes. List type and amount ▶ _ _ _ _ _ _ _ _ _ _ _ _ _ _ _ _	8	
	9	Add lines 5 through 8	9	4,724.
Interest You Paid (See instructions.) **Note.** Personal interest is not deductible.	10	Home mtg interest and points reported to you on Form 1098	10	18,000.
	11	Home mortgage interest not reported to you on Form 1098. If paid to the person from whom you bought the home, see instructions and show that person's name, identifying number, and address ▶ _	11	
	12	Points not reported to you on Form 1098. See instrs for spcl rules	12	
	13	Investment interest. Attach Form 4952 if required. (See instrs.)	13	
	14	Add lines 10 through 13	14	18,000.
Gifts to Charity If you made a gift and got a benefit for it, see instructions.	15	Gifts by cash or check. If you made any gift of $250 or more, see instructions	15	
	16	Other than by cash or check. If any gift of $250 or more, see instructions. You **must** attach Form 8283 if over $500	16	
	17	Carryover from prior year	17	
	18	Add lines 15 through 17	18	
Casualty and Theft Losses	19	Casualty or theft loss(es). Attach Form 4684. (See instructions.)	19	
Job Expenses and Most Other Miscellaneous Deductions (See instructions.)	20	Unreimbursed employee expenses — job travel, union dues, job education, etc. Attach Form 2106 or 2106-EZ if required. (See instructions.) ▶ _	20	
	21	Tax preparation fees	21	
	22	Other expenses — investment, safe deposit box, etc. List type and amount ▶ _ _ _ _ _ _ _ _ _ _ _ _ _ _ _	22	
	23	Add lines 20 through 22	23	
	24	Enter amount from Form 1040, line 37 . . .	24	
	25	Multiply line 24 by 2% (.02)	25	
	26	Subtract line 25 from line 23. If line 25 is more than line 23, enter -0-	26	
Other Miscellaneous Deductions	27	Other — from list in the instructions. List type and amount ▶ _ _ _ _ _ _ _ _ _ _ _ _ _ _	27	
Total Itemized Deductions	28	Is Form 1040, line 37, over $142,700 (over $71,350 if MFS)? ☒ **No.** Your deduction is not limited. Add the amounts in the far right column for lines 4 through 27. Also, enter this amount on Form 1040, line 39. ☐ **Yes.** Your deduction may be limited. See instructions for the amount to enter.	▶ 28	22,724.

BAA For Paperwork Reduction Act Notice, see Form 1040 instructions.   Schedule **A** (Form 1040)

ILLUSTRATION 10.1

SCHEDULE C	**Profit or Loss From Business**	
(Form 1040)	(Sole Proprietorship)	
Department of the Treasury Internal Revenue Service	► Partnerships, joint ventures, etc., must file Form 1065 or 1065-B. ► Attach to Form 1040 or 1041. ► See Instructions for Schedule C (Form 1040).	

Name of proprietor   Social security number (SSN)

JOSEPH HOMEBIZ   070-88-0011

A Principal business or profession, including product or service (see instructions)   **B** Enter code from instructions

CONSULTANT   ► 888888

C Business name. If no separate business name, leave blank.   **D** Employer ID number (EIN), if any

E Business address (including suite or room no.) ► 2200 RODEO DRIVE
City, town or post office, state, and ZIP code   SAINT LOUIS, MO 99999

F Accounting method: (1) [X] Cash   (2) [ ] Accrual   (3) [ ] Other (specify) ►

G Did you 'materially participate' in the operation of this business during   ? If 'No,' see instructions for limit on losses . . . . . [X] Yes [ ] No

H If you started or acquired this business during   , check here . . . . ►

Part I   **Income**

1	Gross receipts or sales. **Caution.** If this income was reported to you on Form W-2 and the 'Statutory employee' box on that form was checked, see the instructions and check here . . . . ► [ ]	1	10,000.
2	Returns and allowances	2	
3	Subtract line 2 from line 1	3	10,000.
4	Cost of goods sold (from line 42 on page 2)	4	
5	**Gross profit.** Subtract line 4 from line 3	5	10,000.
6	Other income, including Federal and state gasoline or fuel tax credit or refund	6	
7	**Gross income.** Add lines 5 and 6 . . . . ►	7	10,000.

Part II   **Expenses.** Enter expenses for business use of your home **only** on line 30.

8	Advertising	8		19	Pension and profit-sharing plans	19	
9	Car and truck expenses (see instructions)	9		20	Rent or lease (see instructions):		
				a	Vehicles, machinery, and equipment	20a	
10	Commissions and fees	10		b	Other business property	20b	
11	Contract labor (see instructions)	11		21	Repairs and maintenance	21	
12	Depletion	12		22	Supplies (not included in Part III)	22	
13	Depreciation and section 179 expense deduction (not included in Part III) (see instructions)	13	2,450.	23	Taxes and licenses	23	
				24	Travel, meals, and entertainment:		
				a	Travel	24a	
14	Employee benefit programs (other than on line 19)	14		b	Meals and entertainment. . .		
15	Insurance (other than health) . .	15		c	Enter nondeductible amount included on line 24b (see instrs) . .		
16	Interest:						
a	Mortgage (paid to banks, etc)	16a		d	Subtract line 24c from line 24b	24d	
b	Other	16b		25	Utilities	25	
17	Legal & professional services . .	17		26	Wages (less employment credits)	26	
18	Office expense	18	4,050.	27	Other expenses (from line 48 on page 2) . .	27	
28	**Total expenses** before expenses for business use of home. Add lines 8 through 27 in columns. . . . . ►					28	6,500.

Transfer from Form 8829 Line 34

29	Tentative profit (loss). Subtract line 28 from line 7	29	3,500.
30	Expenses for business use of your home. Attach **Form 8829**	30	3,500.
31	**Net profit or (loss).** Subtract line 30 from line 29.		
	• If a profit, enter on **Form 1040, line 12,** and also on **Schedule SE, line 2** (statutory employees, see instructions). Estates and trusts, enter on Form 1041, line 3. }.	31	0.
	• If a loss, you **must** go to line 32.		
32	If you have a loss, check the box that describes your investment in this activity (see instructions).		
	• If you checked 32a, enter the loss on **Form 1040, line 12,** and also on **Schedule SE, line 2** (statutory employees, see instructions). Estates and trusts, enter on Form 1041, line 3. }	32a [ ]	All investment is at risk.
		32b [ ]	Some investment is not at risk.
	• If you checked 32b, you **must** attach Form 6198.		

BAA   **For Paperwork Reduction Act Notice, see Form 1040 instructions.**   Schedule C (Form 1040)

ILLUSTRATION 10.1

Schedule **C** (Form 1040)   JOSEPH HOMEBIZ   070-88-0011   Page **2**

Part III   Cost of Goods Sold (see instructions)

33 Method(s) used to value closing inventory: **a** ☐ Cost   **b** ☐ Lower of cost or market   **c** ☐ Other (attach explanation)

34 Was there any change in determining quantities, costs, or valuations between opening and closing inventory?
If 'Yes,' attach explanation . . . . ☐ Yes   ☐ No

35 Inventory at beginning of year. If different from last year's closing inventory, attach explanation	35	
36 Purchases less cost of items withdrawn for personal use	36	
37 Cost of labor. Do not include any amounts paid to yourself	37	
38 Materials and supplies	38	
39 Other costs	39	
40 Add lines 35 through 39	40	
41 Inventory at end of year	41	
42 **Cost of goods sold.** Subtract line 41 from line 40. Enter the result here and on page 1, line 4	42	

Part IV   Information on Your Vehicle. Complete this part **only** if you are claiming car or truck expenses on line 9 and are not required to file Form 4562 for this business. See the instructions for line 13 to find out if you must file Form 4562.

43 When did you place your vehicle in service for business purposes? (month, day, year)   ▶ _ _ _ _ _ _ _ _ _ _ .

44 Of the total number of miles you drove your vehicle during   , enter the number of miles you used your vehicle for:
a Business _ _ _ _ _ _ _ _ _ _   **b** Commuting _ _ _ _ _ _ _ _ _ _   **c** Other _ _ _ _ _ _ _ _ _ _

45 Do you (or your spouse) have another vehicle available for personal use? . . . . ☐ Yes   ☐ No

46 Was your vehicle available for personal use during off-duty hours? . . . . ☐ Yes   ☐ No

47 **a** Do you have evidence to support your deduction? . . . . ☐ Yes   ☐ No

b If 'Yes,' is the evidence written? . . . . ☐ Yes   ☐ No

Part V   Other Expenses. List below business expenses not included on lines 8-26 or line 30.

_____	
_____	
_____	
_____	
_____	
_____	
_____	
_____	
48 **Total other expenses.** Enter here and on page 1, line 27	48

Schedule **C** (Form 1040)

ILLUSTRATION 10.1

Form **8829**	**Expenses for Business Use of Your Home**		
Department of the Treasury Internal Revenue Service	► File only with Schedule C (Form 1040). Use a separate Form 8829 for each home you used for business during the year. ► See separate instructions.		

Name(s) of proprietor(s)		Your social security number
JOSEPH HOMEBIZ	CONSULTANT	070-88-0011

Part I   Part of Your Home Used for Business

1	Area used regularly and exclusively for business, regularly for day care, or for storage of inventory or product samples (see instructions)	1	300
2	Total area of home	2	3,000
3	Divide line 1 by line 2. Enter the result as a percentage	3	10.00 %

• For day-care facilities not used exclusively for business, also complete lines 4 - 6.
• All others, skip lines 4 - 6 and enter the amount from line 3 on line 7.

4	Multiply days used for day care during year by hours used per day	4		hr		
5	Total hours available for use during the year (366 days x 24 hours) (see instructions)	5	8,784	hr		
6	Divide line 4 by line 5. Enter the result as a decimal amount	6				
7	Business percentage. For day-care facilities not used exclusively for business, multiply line 6 by line 3 (enter the result as a percentage). All others, enter the amount from line 3 . . . . ►	7	10.00 %			

Part II   Figure Your Allowable Deduction

8	Enter the amount from Schedule C, line 29, **plus** any net gain or (loss) derived from the business use of your home and shown on Schedule D or Form 4797. If more than one place of business, see instructions.		8	3,500.

	See instrs for columns (a) and (b) before completing lines 9-20.	**(a) Direct expenses**	**(b) Indirect expenses**		
9	Casualty losses (see instructions)	9			
10	Deductible mortgage interest (see instructions)	10	20,000.		
11	Real estate taxes (see instructions).	11	5,000.		
12	Add lines 9, 10, and 11	12	25,000.		
13	Multiply line 12, column (b) by line 7	13	2,500.		
14	Add line 12, column (a) and line 13			14	2,500.
15	Subtract line 14 from line 8. If zero or less, enter -0-			15	1,000.
16	Excess mortgage interest (see instructions)	16			
17	Insurance	17	1,000.		
18	Repairs and maintenance	18	2,000.		
19	Utilities	19	6,000.		
20	Other expenses (see instrs)	20			
21	Add lines 16 through 20	21	9,000.		
22	Multiply line 21, column (b) by line 7	22	900.		
23	Carryover of operating expenses from 2003 Form 8829, line 41	23			
24	Add line 21 in column (a), line 22, and line 23			24	900.
25	Allowable operating expenses. Enter the **smaller** of line 15 or line 24			25	900.
26	Limit on excess casualty losses and depreciation. Subtract line 25 from line 15			26	100.
27	Excess casualty losses (see instructions)	27			
28	Depreciation of your home from Part III below.	28	2,000.		
29	Carryover of excess casualty losses and depreciation from 2003 Form 8829, line 42	29			
30	Add lines 27 through 29			30	2,000.
31	Allowable excess casualty losses and depreciation. Enter the **smaller** of line 26 or line 30			31	100.
32	Add lines 14, 25, and 31			32	3,500.
33	Casualty loss portion, if any, from lines 14 and 31. Carry amount to **Form 4684**, Section B			33	
34	Allowable expenses for business use of your home. Subtract line 33 from line 32. Enter here and on Schedule C, line 30. If your home was used for more than one business, see instructions . . . . ►			34	3,500.

Part III   Depreciation of Your Home

35	Enter the **smaller** of your home's adjusted basis or its fair market value (see instructions)	35	780,000.
36	Value of land included on line 35	36	
37	Basis of building. Subtract line 36 from line 35	37	780,000.
38	Business basis of building. Multiply line 37 by line 7	38	78,000.
39	Depreciation percentage (see instructions)	39	2.5641 %
40	Depreciation allowable (see instructions). Multiply line 38 by line 39. Enter here and on line 28 above	40	2,000.

Part IV   Carryover of Unallowed Expenses

41	Operating expenses. Subtract line 25 from line 24. If less than zero, enter -0-	41	0.
42	Excess casualty losses and depreciation. Subtract line 31 from line 30. If less than zero, enter -0-	42	1,900.

BAA   For Paperwork Reduction Act Notice, see separate instructions.   Form **8829**

Chapter 11

TAX LOOPHOLES

If you plan to sell your rental property, there are a couple of tax loopholes that you may want to consider before you dispose of the property. One popular way to dispose of property with a large gain is through a non-taxable exchange. However, there are conditions that have to be met and failure to meet these conditions will result in you paying taxes on the entire gain.

There is another way that you can sell your rental property and pay little to no taxes, but it requires smart tax planning. Properly executed and depending on your filing status, you may be able to use the $250,000/$500,000 exclusion rules allowed by personal homeowners. Carefully consider which option, if any, best suits your needs. You may have to consult a tax professional for advice.

Non-Taxable Exchange

If your intention is to sell your rental property to acquire another rental property, then you may consider what the IRS calls a deferred exchange. A *deferred exchange* allows you to exchange your rental property for another like-kind rental property.

However, you should understand the true ramifications of a deferred exchange. The first problem with this transaction is that you only delay paying the taxes on any gain that would have been paid if you were to just sell the property.

The second problem with this type of transaction is the time constraints imposed by the IRS to complete the exchange. The IRS wants you to identify the replacement property within forty-five days from the day you gave up your rental property. In addition, you are generally given only 180 days to complete the transaction.

The third problem is that you have to rely on the attorney and real estate agent to meet the IRS's stringent deadlines. There are qualified intermediary companies that can help you with the exchange. However, attorneys and real estate agents are often ignorant about these types of transactions, which is a big problem, since they play the largest role in making sure the exchange is done properly.

Nevertheless, if your intention is to sell your rental property to get another, it really does not make sense to pay the taxes, especially if you have a substantial gain on the property. Find a competent intermediary company and attorney who are familiar with these types of exchanges. Properly done, an exchange can spare you from paying a large tax, at least for now.

Helpful Hint:

To properly execute a deferred exchange, you are not allowed to receive any money from the first property until the second property is properly exchanged. If funds are received before the exchange is fully completed, than the IRS treats the transaction as a sale and will require you to pay taxes. Here is where intermediary companies play a role—they ensure that the funds are properly handled to avoid this type of problem.

Tax Break on Sale of Rental Property

If you decide to sell your rental property and believe the sale will result in a very large tax gain, there may be a true tax loophole that you can take advantage of. If properly planned you may be able to exclude a very large portion of this gain, and it is perfectly legal. You may wonder how this can be done since the IRS only allows you to exclude the gain on the sale of a personal home. The answer is simple—just make your rental property your primary personal residence. This is simple enough, and if done correctly, it can save you a whole lot of money.

To exclude the gain on the sale of your rental property, you must meet certain tests. The property must have been your main home and you must have owned and lived in it at least two years during a period of five years from the date of the sale. In other words, if you met the ownership and use tests any time within five years from the sale, then you may be able to exclude the gain. (See Chapter 3 for a complete discussion.) Single individuals can generally exclude up to a $250,000 gain and married couples filing jointly can exclude up to a $500,000 gain.

If you have not met the test, you must decide whether you would save more by not renting the property and making it your personal residence for the next two years or just selling it as a rental property and paying the gain on the sale. Consult a reputable accountant or tax professional if you are not sure.

There is also one more important factor you have to consider before you decide to convert rental property into your personal residence—depreciation. Although the IRS allows you to exclude the gain if you meet the tests discussed above, it will not allow you to exclude the depreciation you deducted throughout the years on your taxes.

For example, Hector and Libby, who are married filing jointly, sold a rental property that they converted into a personal home. The property was their main home and they met the ownership and use tests. While the property was used for rental purposes they deducted a total of $75,000 in depreciation on their tax returns. The total gain on the property was $400,000. Hector and Libby will have to pay taxes on the first $75,000 and can exclude $325,000 on the remaining gain. See Illustration 11.1.

Determining how to report the gain on a personal residence is all explained in Chapter 3 of this book. Complete Part 2 of Worksheet 2, "Gain (or Loss), Exclusion, and Taxable Gain," to factor in the depreciation that was taken while the property was being used for rental purposes. For further discussion on how to report a personal residence that was used for rental purposes, see IRS Publication 523, "Selling Your Home" at **www.irs.gov**.

ILLUSTRATION 11.1

Form **1040**	Department of the Treasury — Internal Revenue Service	
	U.S. Individual Income Tax Return	

Label (See instructions.)
Use the IRS label. Otherwise, please print or type.

For the year Jan 1 - Dec 31,   , or other tax year beginning   , , ending   , 20

		MI	Last name	Your social security number
Your first name	HECTOR		VILLA	117-34-5678
If a joint return, spouse's first name	LIBBY	MI	Last name VILLA	Spouse's social security number 116-34-5678

Home address (number and street). If you have a P.O. box, see instructions.   Apartment no.
2525 OAK LANE

▲ **Important!** ▲
You **must** enter your social security number(s) above.

City, town or post office. If you have a foreign address. see instructions.   State   ZIP code
OKLAHOMA CITY   OK   00000

Presidential Election Campaign (See instructions.)

▶ **Note:** Checking 'Yes' will not change your tax or reduce your refund.
Do you, or your spouse if filing a joint return, want $3 to go to this fund? . . . . ▶

	You		Spouse	
	Yes	No	Yes	No

Filing Status

Check only one box.

1 ☐ Single
2 ☒ Married filing jointly (even if only one had income)
3 ☐ Married filing separately. Enter spouse's SSN above & full name here. ▶
4 ☐ Head of household (with qualifying person). (See instructions.) If the qualifying person is a child but not your dependent, enter this child's name here ▶
5 ☐ Qualifying widow(er) with dependent child (see instructions)

Exemptions

6a ☒ **Yourself.** If someone can claim you as a dependent, **do not** check box 6a. . . . .
b ☒ **Spouse** . . . .

Boxes checked on 6a and 6b   **2**

c **Dependents:**

(1) First name Last name	(2) Dependent's social security number	(3) Dependent's relationship to you	(4) ✔ if qualifying child for child tax credit (see instrs)
			☐
			☐
			☐
			☐

No. of children on 6c who:
● lived with you . . .
● did not live with you due to divorce or separation (see instrs) . .
Dependents on 6c not entered above . .

If more than four dependents, see instructions.

d Total number of exemptions claimed . . . .

Add numbers on lines above . . . ▶   **2**

Income

Attach Form(s) W-2 here. Also attach Forms W-2G and 1099-R if tax was withheld.

If you did not get a W-2, see instructions.

Enclose, but do not attach, any payment. Also, please use Form 1040-V.

7	Wages, salaries, tips, etc. Attach Form(s) W-2		7	
8a	**Taxable** interest. Attach Schedule B if required		8a	
b	**Tax-exempt** interest. **Do not** include on line 8a	8b		
9a	Ordinary dividends. Attach Schedule B if required		9a	
b	Qualifd divs (see instrs)	9b		
10	Taxable refunds, credits, or offsets of state and local income taxes (see instructions)		10	
11	Alimony received.		11	
12	Business income or (loss). Attach Schedule C or C-EZ		12	
13	Capital gain or (loss). Att Sch D if reqd. If not reqd, ck here . . . . . . ▶ ☐		13	75,000.
14	Other gains or (losses). Attach Form 4797		14	
15a	IRA distributions . . .	15a	b Taxable amount (see instrs) . .	15b	
16a	Pensions and annuities . . .	16a	b Taxable amount (see instrs) . .	16b	
17	Rental real estate, royalties, partnerships, S corporations, trusts, etc. Attach Schedule E . . .		17	
18	Farm income or (loss). Attach Schedule F		18	
19	Unemployment compensation		19	
20a	Social security benefits	20a	b Taxable amount (see instrs) . .	20b	
21	Other income _		21	
22	Add the amounts in the far right column for lines 7 through 21. This is your **total income** . . ▶		22	75,000.

Adjusted Gross Income

23	Educator expenses (see instructions)	23	
24	Certain business expenses of reservists, performing artists, and fee-basis government officials. Attach Form 2106 or 2106-EZ	24	
25	IRA deduction (see instructions)	25	
26	Student loan interest deduction (see instructions)	26	
27	Tuition and fees deduction (see instructions)	27	
28	Health savings account deduction. Attach Form 8889	28	
29	Moving expenses. Attach Form 3903.	29	
30	One-half of self-employment tax. Attach Schedule SE	30	
31	Self-employed health insurance deduction (see instrs)	31	
32	Self-employed SEP, SIMPLE, and qualified plans	32	
33	Penalty on early withdrawal of savings	33	
34a	Alimony paid b Recipient's SSN. . . ▶	34a	
35	Add lines 23 through 34a	35	
36	Subtract line 35 from line 22. This is your **adjusted gross income** . . . . ▶	36	75,000.

BAA For Disclosure, Privacy Act, and Paperwork Reduction Act Notice, see instructions.   Form **1040**

ILLUSTRATION 11.1

Form **1040**	HECTOR & LIBBY VILLA		117-34-5678	Page **2**

Tax and Credits

37	Amount from line 36 (adjusted gross income)	**37**	75,000.

Standard Deduction for —
- People who checked any box on line 38a or 38b **or** who can be claimed as a dependent, see instructions.
- All others:

Single or Married filing separately, $4,850

Married filing jointly or Qualifying widow(er), $9,700

Head of household, $7,150

38a	Check if: ☐ **You** were born before January 2, 1940, ☐ Blind. ☐ **Spouse** was born before January 2, 1940, ☐ Blind. **Total boxes checked** ► **38a**		
b	If your spouse itemizes on a separate return, or you were a dual-status alien, see instructions and check here . . . . ► **38b** ☐		
39	**Itemized deductions** (from Schedule A) or your **standard deduction** (see left margin)	**39**	9,700.
40	Subtract line 39 from line 37	**40**	65,300.
41	If line 37 is $107,025 or less, multiply $3,100 by the total number of exemptions claimed on line 6d. If line 37 is over $107,025, see the worksheet in the instructions	**41**	6,200.
42	**Taxable income.** Subtract line 41 from line 40. If line 41 is more than line 40, enter -0-	**42**	59,100.
43	**Tax** (see instrs). Check if any tax is from: **a** ☐ Form(s) 8814 **b** ☐ Form 4972	**43**	8,256.
44	**Alternative minimum tax** (see instructions). Attach Form 6251	**44**	
45	Add lines 43 and 44 . . . . ►	**45**	8,256.
46	Foreign tax credit. Attach Form 1116 if required	**46**	
47	Credit for child and dependent care expenses. Attach Form 2441	**47**	
48	Credit for the elderly or the disabled. Attach Schedule R	**48**	
49	Education credits. Attach Form 8863	**49**	
50	Retirement savings contributions credit. Attach Form 8880 . . .	**50**	
51	Child tax credit (see instructions)	**51**	
52	Adoption credit. Attach Form 8839	**52**	
53	Credits from: **a** ☐ Form 8396 **b** ☐ Form 8859	**53**	
54	Other credits. Check applicable box(es): **a** ☐ Form 3800 **b** ☐ Form 8801 **c** ☐ Specify	**54**	
55	Add lines 46 through 54. These are your **total credits**	**55**	
56	Subtract line 55 from line 45. If line 55 is more than line 45, enter -0- . . . . ►	**56**	8,256.

Other Taxes

57	Self-employment tax. Attach Schedule SE	**57**	
58	Social security and Medicare tax on tip income not reported to employer. Attach Form 4137	**58**	
59	Additional tax on IRAs, other qualified retirement plans, etc. Attach Form 5329 if required	**59**	
60	Advance earned income credit payments from Form(s) W-2	**60**	
61	Household employment taxes. Attach Schedule H	**61**	
62	Add lines 56-61. This is your **total tax** . . . . ►	**62**	8,256.

Payments

If you have a qualifying child, attach Schedule EIC.

63	Federal income tax withheld from Forms W-2 and 1099	**63**	
64	2004 estimated tax payments and amount applied from 2003 return	**64**	8,256.
65a	**Earned income credit (EIC)**.	**65a**	
b	Nontaxable combat pay election . . . ►	**65b**	
66	Excess social security and tier 1 RRTA tax withheld (see instructions) . . .	**66**	
67	Additional child tax credit. Attach Form 8812	**67**	
68	Amount paid with request for extension to file (see instructions)	**68**	
69	Other pmts from: **a** ☐ Form 2439 **b** ☐ Form 4136 **c** ☐ Form 8885	**69**	
70	Add lines 63, 64, 65a, and 66 through 69. These are your **total payments** . . . . ►	**70**	8,256.

Refund

Direct deposit? See instructions and fill in 72b, 72c, and 72d.

71	If line 70 is more than line 62, subtract line 62 from line 70. This is the amount you **overpaid**	**71**	
72a	Amount of line 71 you want **refunded to you** . . . . ►	**72a**	
► b	Routing number . . . . . ► **c** Type: ☐ Checking ☐ Savings		
► d	Account number		
73	Amount of line 71 you want **applied to your 2005 estimated tax** . . . . ►	**73**	

Amount You Owe

74	**Amount you owe.** Subtract line 70 from line 62. For details on how to pay, see instructions . . . . ►	**74**	0.
75	Estimated tax penalty (see instructions)	**75**	

Third Party Designee

Do you want to allow another person to discuss this return with the IRS (see instructions)? . . . . . . ☐ **Yes.** Complete the following. ☒ **No**

Designee's name ►	Phone no. ►	Personal identification number (PIN) ►

Sign Here

Joint return? See instructions.

Keep a copy for your records.

Under penalties of perjury, I declare that I have examined this return and accompanying schedules and statements, and to the best of my knowledge and belief, they are true, correct, and complete. Declaration of preparer (other than taxpayer) is based on all information of which preparer has any knowledge.

Your signature ►	Date	Your occupation GW	Daytime phone number
Spouse's signature. If a joint return, **both** must sign. ►	Date	Spouse's occupation GW	

Paid Preparer's Use Only

Preparer's signature ► Self-Prepared	Date	Check if self-employed ☐	Preparer's SSN or PTIN
Firm's name (or yours if self-employed), address, and ZIP code ►		EIN Phone no.	

Form **1040**

ILLUSTRATION 11.1

SCHEDULE D						
(Form 1040)		Capital Gains and Losses				

► Attach to Form 1040.   ► See Instructions for Schedule D (Form 1040).
► Use Schedule D-1 to list additional transactions for lines 1 and 8.

Name(s) shown on Form 1040: HECTOR & LIBBY VILLA

Your social security number: 117-34-5678

Part I   Short-Term Capital Gains and Losses — Assets Held One Year or Less

(a) Description of property (Example: 100 shares XYZ Co)	(b) Date acquired (Mo, day, yr)	(c) Date sold (Mo, day, yr)	(d) Sales price (see instructions)	(e) Cost or other basis (see instructions)	(f) Gain or (loss) Subtract (e) from (d)
1					

2 Enter your short-term totals, if any, from Schedule D-1, line 2 . . . . | **2** |

3 Total short-term sales price amounts. Add lines 1 and 2 in column (d) . . . . | **3** |

4 Short-term gain from Form 6252 and short-term gain or (loss) from Forms 4684, 6781, and 8824 . . . . | **4** |

5 Net short-term gain or (loss) from partnerships, S corporations, estates, and trusts from Schedule(s) K-1 . . . . . | **5** |

6 Short-term capital loss carryover. Enter the amount, if any, from line 8 of your **Capital Loss Carryover Worksheet** in the instructions . . . . | **6** |

7 **Net short-term capital gain or (loss).** Combine lines 1 through 6 in column (f) . . . . | **7** |

Part II   Long-Term Capital Gains and Losses — Assets Held More Than One Year

(a) Description of property (Example: 100 shares XYZ Co)	(b) Date acquired (Mo, day, yr)	(c) Date sold (Mo, day, yr)	(d) Sales price (see instructions)	(e) Cost or other basis (see instructions)	(f) Gain or (loss) Subtract (e) from (d)
8 Home Sale Gain Realized			500,000.	100,000.	400,000.
Section 121 Exclusion					-325,000.

Cannot Exclude Depreciation

9 Enter your long-term totals, if any, from Schedule D-1, line 9 . . . . . | **9** |

10 Total long-term sales price amounts. Add lines 8 and 9 in column (d) . . . . | **10** | 500,000. |

11 Gain from Form 4797, Part I; long-term gain from Forms 2439 and 6252; and long-term gain or (loss) from Forms 4684, 6781, and 8824 . . . . | **11** |

12 Net long-term gain or (loss) from partnerships, S corporations, estates, and trusts from Schedule(s) K-1 . . . . . | **12** |

13 Capital gain distributions. See instrs . . . . | **13** |

14 Long-term capital loss carryover. Enter the amount, if any, from line 13 of your **Capital Loss Carryover Worksheet** in the instructions . . . . | **14** |

15 **Net long-term capital gain or (loss).** Combine lines 8 through 14 in column (f). Then go to Part III on page 2 . . . . | **15** | 75,000. |

Schedule D (Form 1040)

ILLUSTRATION 11.1

| Schedule D (Form 1040) | HECTOR & LIBBY VILLA | 117-34-5678 | Page **2** |

Part III   Summary

16 Combine lines 7 and 15 and enter the result. If line 16 is a loss, skip lines 17 through 20, and go to line 21.
If a gain, enter the gain on Form 1040, line 13, and then go to line 17 below . . . . **16** 75,000.

17 Are lines 15 and 16 **both** gains?

[X] **Yes.** Go to line 18.

[ ] **No.** Skip lines 18 through 21, and go to line 22.

18 Enter the amount, if any, from line 7 of the **28% Rate Gain Worksheet** in the instructions . . . . ▶ **18**

19 Enter the amount, if any, from line 18 of the **Unrecaptured Section 1250 Gain Worksheet** in
the instructions . . . . ▶ **19** 75,000.

20 Are lines 18 and 19 **both** zero or blank?

[ ] **Yes.** Complete Form 1040 through line 42, and then complete the **Qualified Dividends and Capital Gain Tax Worksheet** in the instructions for Form 1040. **Do not** complete lines 21 and 22 below.

[X] **No.** Complete Form 1040 through line 42, and then complete the **Schedule D Tax Worksheet** in the instructions. **Do not** complete lines 21 and 22 below.

21 If line 16 is a loss, enter here and on Form 1040, line 13, the **smaller** of:

- The loss on line 16 or
- ($3,000), or if married filing separately, ($1,500) **21**

Note. When figuring which amount is smaller, treat both amounts as positive numbers.

22 Do you have qualified dividends on Form 1040, line 9b?

[ ] **Yes.** Complete Form 1040 through line 42, and then complete the **Qualified Dividends and Capital Gain Tax Worksheet** in the Instructions for Form 1040.

[ ] **No.** Complete the rest of Form 1040.

Schedule **D** (Form 1040)

GLOSSARY

A

adjusted cost. The purchase price adjusted by certain closing and other home costs.

adjusted selling price. The contract sales price less certain selling expenses.

C

closing costs. Fees charged during the purchase of a home and paid at closing. See also *settlement fees*.

condominium. The ownership of a dwelling unit in a housing complex that shares certain common areas, such as elevators and lobbies.

cooperative (co-op). The ownership of housing stock that entitles an individual to live in one of the units.

D

deferred exchange. A tax-free exchange of property for like-kind property.

depreciation. A method to deduct certain large expenses over a period of time opposed to when they were paid.

H

home equity. The difference between what a home is worth and what is owed on the home.

improvement. An expense that adds value to the home, extends the useful life of what was improved, or adapts the home to new changes.

itemized deduction. Certain deductible personal expenses that reduce taxable income.

M

maintenance fees. Fees charged to co-op and condominium owners to pay for the upkeep of the dwelling complex, real estate taxes, and loans.

mortgage. A loan taken out by homebuyers and usually paid back on a monthly basis.

mortgage interest. The amount charged to homebuyers in exchange for lending them money.

P

passive activities. Income-producing activities that take little to no effort to perform.

points. An up-front fee charged by the lending institution that allows lenders to borrow at a lower interest rate.

private mortgage insurance (PMI). An insurance policy that bridges the gap between what a house is worth and what is owed in case of foreclosure.

R

real estate taxes. Fees charged by the state or local government, based on the value of the property.

refianace. To replace the old mortgage with a new one.

repair. An expense that keeps the home in good working order.

reverse mortgage. Programs for seniors age 62 and over that allow them to receive money against the equity of their home.

S

settlement fees. Fees charged during the purchase of a home and paid at closing.

standard deduction. A fixed personal deduction based on a taxpayer's filing status.

T

tax deduction. Certain expenses that that reduce taxable income.

trade down. To sell your larger home for a smaller home.

Appendix A

Tax Treatment of Personal Home by Each State

So far all that you have learned on the tax rules for purchasing, owning, and selling a personal home are rules promulgated by the federal government through the Internal Revenue Tax Code. These rules dictate what, when, and where to report income and deductions. However, for most people the IRS Form 1040 is not the only tax return that has to be filed. Most states require that you report and pay taxes on the same income that is reported on your federal tax return, and if that is not enough, there are a few localities (like New York City) that want a piece of the action.

The following table guides you on what states allow deductions for mortgage interest and property taxes, and those states that require you to report and pay taxes on the gain from the sale of a personal residence. Be advised that there is no need to perform complex calculations to determine the gain on a home—simply use the amount of gain reported on your federal tax return. For example, if you determine that after the exclusion the taxable gain from the sale of a personal home under federal rules is $45,000 and you are required to report the gain in the state, you would use the same amount.

The way each state assesses personal income taxes is very dynamic. The table guides you on what to deduct and report for each state, but be aware that even though you are allowed a deduction in one state and not the other, the tax rates for the state that allows the deduction compared to the state that does not could be much higher, causing you to pay more taxes on the same amount of income. Do not think that one state is better than another until you analyze the tax rates (unless you live in a state like Florida, which does not tax personal income).

Appendix A: Tax Treatment of Personal Home by Each State

State	Mortgage Interest	Property Taxes	Gain on Sale	Comments
Alabama	Deductible	Deductible	Taxable	
Alaska	Not Applicable	Not Applicable	Not Applicable	Personal income is not taxed in Alaska, so income, gains, and deductions are not reportable and the sale of a personal home is not taxable.
Arizona	Deductible	Deductible	Taxable	
Arkansas	Deductible	Deductible	Partially Taxable	Only 70% of the gain from the sale of a personal home is taxable in the state of Arkansas. Refer to form AR1000D for the most updated information on this amount.
California	Deductible	Deductible	Taxable	
Colorado	Deductible	Deductible	Taxable	
Connecticut	Non-Deductible	Tax Credit	Taxable	Instead of a real estate tax deduction, a small tax credit is allowed.
Delaware	Deductible	Deductible	Taxable	
District of Columbia	Deductible	Deductible	Taxable	
Florida	Not Applicable	Not Applicable	Not Applicable	Personal income is not taxed in Florida, so income, gains, and deductions are not reportable and the sale of a personal home is not taxable.

Georgia	Deductible	Deductible	Taxable	
Hawaii	Deductible	Deductible	Taxable	Hawaii uses capital gain tax rates to assess the amount of tax owed from the sale of a personal home.
Idaho	Deductible	Deductible	Taxable	
Illinois	Non-Deductible	Tax Credit	Taxable	Instead of a real estate tax deduction, a small tax credit is allowed.
Indiana	Non-Deductible	Deductible (limited)	Taxable	Real estate tax deductions cannot exceed the established ceiling amount of $2,500. Refer to form Schedule 1 for the most updated information on this deduction.
Indiana County Tax	Non-Deductible	Deductible (limited)	Taxable	In addition to Indiana state taxes, residents are required to pay applicable county taxes.
Iowa	Deductible	Deductible	Taxable	
Kansas	Deductible	Deductible	Taxable	
Kentucky	Deductible	Deductible	Taxable	
Louisiana	Non-Deductible	Non-Deductible	Taxable	
Maine	Deductible	Deductible	Taxable	
Maryland	Deductible	Deductible	Taxable	
Maryland County Tax	Deductible	Deductible	Taxable	In addition to Maryland state taxes, residents are required to pay applicable county taxes.

Massachusetts	Non-Deductible	Non-Deductible	Taxable	Massachusetts uses capital gain tax rates to assess the amount of tax owed from the sale of a personal home.
Michigan	Non-Deductible	Non-Deductible	Taxable	
Minnesota	Deductible	Deductible	Taxable	
Mississippi	Deductible	Deductible	Taxable	
Missouri	Deductible	Deductible	Taxable	
Montana	Deductible	Deductible	Taxable	Montana allows individuals to reduce the total state taxes owed by 1% of the capital gain amount from the sale of a personal home. (A capital gain tax credit of 1%.)
Nebraska	Deductible	Deductible	Taxable	
Nevada	Not Applicable	Not Applicable	Not Applicable	Personal income is not taxed in Nevada, so income, gains, and deductions are not reportable and the sale of a personal home is not taxable.
New Hampshire	Not Applicable	Not Applicable	Not Applicable	Most income is not reportable or taxed in New Hampshire. Mortgage interest and property taxes are not reportable and the gain on the sale is not taxable.

New Jersey	Non-Deductible	Deductible	Taxable	
New Mexico	Deductible	Deductible	Taxable	New Mexico allows a 30% deduction based on the capital gain from the sale of a personal home. This deduction reduces the total amount of taxable income. Refer to Schedule PIT-ADJ for the most updated information on this deduction.
New York State	Deductible	Deductible	Taxable	
New York City	Deductible	Deductible	Taxable	In addition to New York state taxes, New York City residents of Brooklyn, Bronx, Queens, Manhattan, or Staten Island are responsible for New York City resident taxes.
North Carolina	Deductible	Deductible	Taxable	

North Dakota	Deductible	Deductible	Taxable	North Dakota allows a 30% deduction based on the capital gain from the sale of a personal home. This deduction reduces the total amount of taxable income. Refer to Form ND-1 for the most updated information on this deduction.
Ohio	Non-Deductible	Non-Deductible	Taxable	
Ohio Municipal Tax	Non-Deductible	Non-Deductible	Not Applicable	In addition to an Ohio state return, a municipal tax return must be filed. The taxes are assessed on certain income, but excludes any tax on the gain from the sale of a home.
Oklahoma	Deductible	Deductible	Taxable	
Oregon	Deductible	Deductible	Taxable	
Multnomah County	Deductible	Deductible	Taxable	In addition to Oregon state tax, applicable Multnomah County taxes must be paid.

Pennsylvania	Non-Deductible	Non-Deductible	Non-Taxable	Generally, if you pass all the tests to exclude the gain for federal purposes, the entire gain is excludible in Pennsylvania.
Rhode Island	Deductible	Deductible	Taxable	Rhode Island uses capital gain tax rates to assess the amount of taxes owed from the sale of a personal home.
South Carolina	Deductible	Deductible	Taxable	
South Dakota	Not Applicable	Not Applicable	Not Applicable	Personal income is not taxed in South Dakota, so income, gains, and deductions are not reportable and the sale of a personal home is not taxable.
Tennessee	Not Applicable	Not Applicable	Not Applicable	Most income is not taxed in Tennessee, so income, gains, and deductions are not reportable and the sale of a personal home is not taxable.
Texas	Not Applicable	Not Applicable	Not Applicable	Personal income is not taxed in Texas, so income, gains, and deductions are not reportable and the sale of a personal home is not taxable.

Utah	Deductible	Deductible	Taxable	
Vermont	Deductible	Deductible	Partially Taxable	Vermont allows a 40% deduction based on the capital gain from the sale of a personal home. This deduction reduces the total amount of taxable income. Refer to form IN-111 for the most updated information on this deduction.
Virginia	Deductible	Deductible	Taxable	
Washington	Not Applicable	Not Applicable	Not Applicable	Personal income is not taxed in Washington, so income, gains, and deductions are not reportable and the sale of a personal home is not taxable.
West Virginia	Non-Deductible	Non-Deductible	Taxable	

Wisconsin	Tax Credit	Tax Credit	Partially Taxable	Instead of a mortgage and property tax deduction, a credit is given to offset the tax liability. In addition, Wisconsin allows a 60% deduction based on the capital gain from the sale of a personal home. This deduction reduces the total amount of taxable income. Refer to form Schedule WD for the most updated information on this deduction.
Wyoming	Not Applicable	Not Applicable	Not Applicable	Personal income is not taxed in Wyoming, so income, gains, and deductions are not reportable and the gain on the sale is not taxable.

Appendix B

TAX TREATMENT OF RESIDENTIAL RENTAL PROPERTY BY EACH STATE

So far all that you have learned on the tax rules for purchasing, owning, and selling residential rental property are rules promulgated by the federal government through the Internal Revenue Tax Code. These rules dictate how to report rental activities. However, for most people the IRS Form 1040 is not the only tax return that has to be filed. Most states require that you report and pay taxes on the same income that is reported on your federal tax return, and if that is not enough there are a few localities (like New York City) that want a piece of the action.

The following table guides you on what states allow deductions for mortgage interest and property taxes, and those states that require you to report rental income and expenses, allow you to deduct rental losses, and require you to pay taxes on the gain from the sale of rental property. Be advised that there is no need to perform complex calculations to determine the gain on a home—simply use the amount of gain reported on your federal tax return. For example, if you determine that the taxable gain from the sale of rental property under federal rules is $20,000 and you are required to report the gain in your state, you would use the same amount.

The way each state assesses personal income taxes is very dynamic. The table guides you on what to deduct and report for each state, but be aware that even though you are allowed a deduction in one state and not the other, the tax rates for the state that allows the deduction compared to the state that does not could be much higher, causing you to pay more taxes on the same amount of income. Do not think that one state is better than another until you analyze the tax rates (unless you live in a state like Florida, which does not tax personal income).

Appendix B: Tax Treatment of Residential Rental Property by Each State

State	Rental Income & Expenses	Rental Loss	Gain On Sale	Comments
Alabama	Reportable	Deductible	Taxable	
Alaska	Not Applicable	Not Applicable	Not Applicable	Personal income is not taxed in Alaska, so rental activities are not reportable and the gain from the sale of rental property is not taxable.
Arizona	Reportable	Deductible	Taxable	
Arkansas	Reportable	Deductible	Partially Taxable	Only 70% of the gain from the sale of rental property is taxable in the state of Arkansas. Refer to form AR1000D for the most updated information on this amount.
Connecticut	Reportable	Deductible	Taxable	
California	Reportable	Deductible	Taxable	
Colorado	Reportable	Deductible	Taxable	
Delaware	Reportable	Deductible	Taxable	
District of Columbia	Reportable	Deductible	Taxable	
Florida	Not Applicable	Not Applicable	Not Applicable	Personal income is not taxed in Florida, so rental activities are not reportable and the gain from the sale of rental property is not taxable.
Georgia	Reportable	Deductible	Taxable	

Hawaii	Reportable	Deductible	Taxable	Hawaii uses capital gain tax rates to assess the amount of tax owed from the sale of rental property.
Idaho	Reportable	Deductible	Taxable	Idaho allows a 60% deduction based on the capital gain from the sale of rental property. This deduction reduces the total amount of taxable income. Refer to form CG for the most updated information on this deduction.
Illinois	Reportable	Deductible	Taxable	
Indiana	Reportable	Deductible	Taxable	
Indiana County Tax	Reportable	Deductible	Taxable	In addition to a Indiana state tax, residents are required to pay applicable county taxes.
Iowa	Reportable	Deductible	Taxable	
Kansas	Reportable	Deductible	Taxable	
Kentucky	Reportable	Deductible	Taxable	
Louisiana	Reportable	Deductible	Taxable	
Maine	Reportable	Deductible	Taxable	
Maryland	Reportable	Deductible	Taxable	
Maryland County Tax	Reportable	Deductible	Taxable	In addition to Maryland state taxes, residents are required to pay applicable county taxes.

Massachusetts	Reportable	Deductible	Taxable	Massachusetts uses capital gain tax rates to assess the amount of tax owed from the sale of rental property.
Michigan	Reportable	Deductible	Taxable	
Minnesota	Reportable	Deductible	Taxable	
Mississippi	Reportable	Deductible	Taxable	
Missouri	Reportable	Deductible	Taxable	
Montana	Reportable	Deductible	Taxable	Montana allows individuals to reduce the total state taxes owed by 1% of the capital gain amount from the sale of rental property. (A capital gain tax credit of 1%.)
Nebraska	Reportable	Deductible	Taxable	
Nevada	Not Applicable	Not Applicable	Not Applicable	Personal income is not taxed in Nevada, so rental activities are not reportable and the gain from the sale of rental property is not taxable.
New Hampshire	Not Applicable	Not Applicable	Not Applicable	Most income is not reportable or taxed in New Hampshire. Rental activities are not reportable and the gain from the sale of rental property is not taxable.

New Jersey	Reportable	Non-Deductible	Taxable	New Jersey requires the reporting of rental activities and requires that rental profit be included as taxable income; however, it does not allow a deduction for a rental loss.
New Mexico	Reportable	Deductible	Taxable	New Mexico allows a 30% deduction based on the capital gain from the sale of rental property. This deduction reduces the total amount of taxable income. Refer to Schedule PIT-ADJ for the most updated information on this deduction.
New York State	Reportable	Deductible	Taxable	
New York City	Reportable	Deductible	Taxable	In addition to New York state tax, New York City residents of Brooklyn, Bronx, Queens, Manhattan, or Staten Island are responsible for New York City resident taxes.
North Carolina	Reportable	Deductible	Taxable	

North Dakota	Reportable	Deductible	Taxable	North Dakota allows a 30% deduction based on the capital gain from the sale of rental property. This deduction reduces the total amount of taxable income. Refer to Form ND-1 for the most updated information on this deduction.
Ohio	Reportable	Deductible	Taxable	
Ohio Municipal Tax	Reportable	It Depends	Taxable	In addition to an Ohio state tax, a municipal tax may be assessed on certain income including rental income. Rental losses are not deductible by itself, but can offset certain other income such as the gain on the sale of rental property. See applicable municipal tax forms for specific instructions.
Oklahoma	Reportable	Deductible	Taxable	
Oregon	Reportable	Deductible	Taxable	
Multnomah County	Reportable	Deductible	Taxable	In addition to Oregon state tax, applicable Multnomah County taxes must be paid.

Pennsylvania	Reportable	Non-Deductible	Taxable	Rental losses are not deductible.
Rhode Island	Reportable	Deductible	Taxable	Rhode Island uses capital gain tax rates to assess the amount of taxes owed from the sale of rental property.
South Carolina	Reportable	Deductible	Taxable	
South Dakota	Not Applicable	Not Applicable	Not Applicable	Personal income is not taxed in South Dakota, so rental activities are not reportable and the gain from the sale of rental property is not taxable.
Tennessee	Not Applicable	Not Applicable	Not Applicable	Most income is not taxed in Tennessee, so rental activities are not reportable and the gain from the sale of rental property is not taxable.
Texas	Not Applicable	Not Applicable	Not Applicable	Personal income is not taxed in Texas, so rental activities are not reportable and the gain from the sale of rental property is not taxable.
Utah	Reportable	Deductible	Taxable	

Vermont	Reportable	Deductible	Taxable	Vermont allows a 40% deduction based on the capital gain from the sale of rental property. This deduction reduces the total amount of taxable income. Refer to form IN-111 for the most updated information on this deduction.
Virginia	Reportable	Deductible	Taxable	
Washington	Not Applicable	Not Applicable	Not Applicable	Personal income is not taxed in Washington, so rental activities are not reportable and the gain from the sale of rental property is not taxable.
West Virginia	Reportable	Deductible	Taxable	
Wisconsin	Reportable	Deductible	Taxable	Wisconsin allows a 60% deduction based on the capital gain from the sale of rental property. This deduction reduces the total amount of taxable income. Refer to form Schedule WD for the most updated information on this deduction.

Wyoming	Not Applicable	Not Applicable	Not Applicable	Personal income is not taxed in Wyoming, so rental activities are not reportable and the gain from the sale of rental property is not taxable.

INDEX

S

T

U

V

ABOUT THE AUTHOR

Robert L. Balducci received his BBA with honors from the Bernard M. Baruch College of the City University of New York and is a Certified Public Accountant currently licensed to practice in the state of New York.

Mr. Balducci has a diverse accounting career working in banking, retail, medical, and government industries. He has spent the last thirteen years supervising government audits that uncovered fraud, waste, and inappropriate accounting practices. He currently serves as the Chief Quality Assurance Officer over the City of New York accounting and financial reporting systems.

His true passion and love is his accounting and tax practice, which was founded in 1994. Starting with 200 clients, his practice has grown to over 2,000 strong. While serving his clients, he noticed that his clients had a need to become educated and guided in many personal financial decisions, including buying or selling real estate. Even though the faces were different, they seemed to ask him all the same questions. He may have not seen it all, but he has seen enough to offer expert advice to his clients. Through his consulting and guidance he has protected his clients from the expensive shortfalls of making bad personal finance decisions.

Mr. Balducci's goal is to educate, advise, and share his experiences beyond his clientele.